Start Your Own

LAW PRACTICE

Additional titles in *Entrepreneur's* **Startup Series**

Start Your Own

- Bar and Tavern
- Bed & Breakfast
- Business on eBay
- Business Support Service
- Car Wash
- Child Care Service
- Cleaning Service
- Clothing Store
- Coin-Operated Laundry
- Consulting
- Crafts Business
- e-Business
- e-Learning Business
- Event Planning Business
- Executive Recruiting Service
- Freight Brokerage Business
- Gift Basket Service
- Growing and Selling Herbs and Herbal Products
- Home Inspection Service
- Import/Export Business
- Information Consultant Business
- Lawn Care Business
- Mail Order Business
- Medical Claims Billing Service
- Personal Concierge Service
- Personal Training Business
- Pet-Sitting Business
- Restaurant and Five Other Food Businesses
- Self-Publishing Business
- Seminar Production Business
- Specialty Travel & Tour Business
- Staffing Service
- Successful Retail Business
- Vending Business
- Wedding Consultant Business
- Wholesale Distribution Business

Entrepreneur MAGAZINE'S

startup

Start Your Own

LAW PRACTICE

Your Step-by-Step Guide to Success

Entrepreneur Press and Laura Valtorta

Ep
Entrepreneur Press

Editorial Director: Jere L. Calmes
Managing Editor: Marla Markman
Cover Design: Beth Hansen-Winter

© 2005 by Entrepreneur Media, Inc.
All rights reserved.
Reproduction or translation of any part of this work beyond that permitted by Section 107 or 108 of the 1976 United States Copyright Act without permission of the copyright owner is unlawful. Requests for permission or further information should be addressed to the Business Products Division, Entrepreneur Media Inc.

This publication is designed to provide accurate and authoritative information in regard to the subject matter covered. It is sold with the understanding that the publisher is not engaged in rendering legal, accounting or other professional services. If legal advice or other expert assistance is required, the services of a competent professional person should be sought.

Library of Congress Cataloging-in-Publication Data

Valtorta, Laura P., 1958–.
    Start your own law practice/by Laura P. Valtorta.
      p.   cm.   —(Startup)
    ISBN 1-932531-31-9 (alk. paper)
      1. Solo law practice—United States. I. Title. II. Startup series.

KF300.V35 2005
340'.023'73—dc21
                                                                                         2005009372

Printed in Canada

Contents

Preface ix

Chapter 1
Early Decisions 1
   The Relevance of Law School 2
   Having the Right Stuff to Go Solo 4
      The Rules 5
      Working on Your Own 5
      Money 5
      A Strong Desire to Help People 6
      The Ability to Listen and Empathize 6
      A Force for Change 6
   Partnerships 8
   Dispelling Myths about Lawyers:
      Dead Snakes and Evildoers 10
      Don't Steal the Clients' Money 10
      Don't Misuse Your Power 11
      Stick to the Truth 12
      Avoid Conflicts of Interest 13
   Choosing the Right Areas of Practice 14
      First Choice: The Passion 15

      Second Choice: The Old Standard............................ 15
      Third Choice: Lucrative Relaxation........................... 16

Chapter 2
Your Office... **19**
   Style of the Office: Projecting an Image........................ 20
   Accessibility... 20
   Location, Location, Location...................................... 21

Chapter 3
Getting Started.. **23**
   Business License.. 24
   Incorporation.. 24
   Liability Insurance... 24
   Office Equipment and Record-Keeping....................... 25
      Files.. 26
      Computers and their Programs........................... 27
      Printers.. 27
      Copiers.. 27
      Telephone Systems and Internet Connections..... 28
   Law Books... 28
      Bank Accounts.. 29
      Basic Forms.. 30

Chapter 4
Frugality... **33**
   Employees.. 34
      Know the Law... 35
      Be Smart... 35
   Financing.. 36
   How Much to Charge.. 37
   Advertising... 38
      Telephone Book Ads.. 39
      State Bar Referral Service................................. 39
      What to Avoid... 39

Chapter 5
What They Don't Teach You in Law School............ **41**
   Mentors: You've Got to Have Them........................... 42
   Managing a Case... 44

Retainer Agreement. 45
Creating a File 45
Keeping a Case Alive 47
Client Control and Settlement 48

Chapter 6
Settling Outside of Court. 51
The Benefits of Settlement 52
The Negotiated Settlement 53
    Mediation. 54
    Arbitration 55

Chapter 7
Playing Well with Others. 57
Relationships with Other Professionals 58
    Doctors. 58
    Social Workers and Therapists 60
    Accountants 60
    Law Enforcement Officials 61
Relationships with Legal Professionals. 62
    Clerks of Court 62
    Your Peers 63
    The Benefits of Networking 63
    Developing Connections. 64

Chapter 8
Using the Library and the Internet 67

Chapter 9
Get a Life. 71
Time Management for Work 72
Balancing the Books 73
Scheduling Non-Work Activities 73

Chapter 10
Representing Clients. 75
Client Control 76
    Client Who Thinks He's a Lawyer. 76
    Vengeful Client 77
    Compound Client 78

    Mother–Daughter Compound Client. 79
    Client with Money Problems 79
    Sick Client 80
    Addicted Client 80
    Mentally Ill Client. 81
    Physically Ill Client 82
    Client Who Needs Multiple Services. 82
    Persistent Client 83
    Humorous Client. 84
Clients on Stage: Depositions 84

Chapter 11
Theories about Practicing Law 87
Therapeutic Jurisprudence 88
Preparing the Client 88
Handling Emotions 90
    Assessing the Law 91
Shaping Public Policy 92
    Changing the Laws 93
    The Benefits of Public Service 94
Behaving Well in Court. 94
    Staying Cool 94
    How to Stay Cool 95
    Dress for Success. 96
    Acknowledging the Court Reporter 97
Handicapped but Not Disabled 97
    Accessibility 98
Conclusion: The Compleat Lawyer 99
    Acknowledging the Client's Stress 99
    The Client's Financial Problems. 99
    The Client's Psychological Problems 100
    Listening to the Client 100
    Accepting the Responsibilities of the Law 101

Appendix
Helpful Resources 103

Glossary 109

Index 111

Preface

Let's face it, lawyers, as a group, have a bad reputation. From Shakespeare's *Henry IV* ("First get rid of all the lawyers") to comparisons with devils and poisonous snakes, lawyers bear the brunt of many people's complaints about modern society.

Finding a Voice

This image is unfortunate because lawyers have the power to help just about anyone navigate the legal system, conduct better business, exercise civil rights, get out of jail, demand justice, change the laws, and generally live better lives. Lawyers have great power to do good deeds because they understand how the system works. They can guide people through difficult and tragic times in their lives. They can advise their clients to do the right thing. In short, lawyers, more often than not, are the good guys in the white hats.

Solo and small firm practitioners, even more than corporate counsel, government lawyers, or large firm practitioners, have the opportunity to make direct, positive changes in people's lives. This is because lawyers in small firms work on the front line. They interact with their clients personally, on a daily basis, on the telephone, over the internet, and in the office. Their clients are the people and the small businesses who cannot afford help from the larger firms. Small practitioners often have the responsibility of leveling the playing field when individuals run up against their employers, their spouses, or the legal system itself. This is a huge task, and one that should not be undertaken by lawyers who have a negative attitude toward the poor, the disadvantaged, or the temporarily insane. As many family lawyers will tell you, many divorce clients become difficult to deal with during the duration of the case.

This book is as a manual, a warning device, and a descriptive tool for lawyers or law students thinking of hanging up a shingle. It includes practical advice, money-saving hints, and a picture of small practice lawyering not touched on in law school. This lack of complete education is not necessarily a good thing for the profession. Law school only teaches legal research, how to read cases. It also needs to include compulsory, paid internships, and a variety of practical courses in which students handle cases under the guidance of practicing attorneys.

A particularly glaring gap in the education of lawyers is the failure to include courses on psychology, sociology, and public policy, which are useful in the real world of law. Practicing attorneys, especially those in small offices, face the glaring problems of society on a daily basis. If illegal drugs are a huge problem, dragging communities down, attorneys see the problem in their offices face-to-face, along with all the peripheral headaches that plague the addict and her family. If lack of universal health insurance is a conundrum that needs to be addressed, attorneys in small practices see how lack of good medical care affects their clients. Attorneys in small firms regularly deal with both legal and social questions.

Most lawyers describe themselves as "attorneys and counselors at law." The "counselor" part is no joke. People who seek legal advice often have mental, economic, and social problems that are staggering. Treating the client's legal problems necessarily involves looking at their other assorted problems, the people in their families, their educational deficiencies, and their living conditions in general. What can be done to help? One approach,

The Whole Truth
Lawyers have the power to improve people's lives.

therapeutic jurisprudence, entails considering the client's entire situation, rather than one isolated legal problem. How does the law and the judicial system affect this client's emotional health?

Sometimes all the lawyer can do is to consider the client's situation: nothing much can be done besides obtaining Social Security benefits, plea bargaining, or getting the parties divorced and praying they avoid each other afterwards. But by considering the client's entire situation, the lawyer can discover patterns in society, flaws in the system, and situations that ought to be changed in order to help a large part of the population. These observations lead to theories. Theories lead to public policy arguments. Lawyers from all sides of the political spectrum who work on their own and are beholden to no one (other than the bar and their clients) can form educated opinions and lobby the government for change. These lawyers can make things happen.

This book is as much a celebration of small firm practice and its roller-coaster lifestyle as it is a practical guide. It's a celebration of the lawyers, their mentors, and their support staff, people who ought to be known as the good guys and gals rather than the snakes.

But enough mushy philosophy. The truth is that lawyers can become whatever they choose. Some clients need hired guns. The law encompasses a wide range of beliefs, 360-degrees of ethical orientations, and a wide variety of talent. It is a profession suitable for quiet scholars and confrontational courtroom orators, conservatives and liberals. Some lawyers wouldn't be seen outside—weekend or week day—without a button-down shirt or high-heeled shoes. Other lawyers dress very informally. A lawyer can be whatever she wants to be, as long as she is smart and dedicated. Freedom is the beauty of this profession.

Perhaps the freest lawyer of all is the solo practitioner, followed closely by the small partnership. Not free in terms of money—because only the luckiest can expect a lavish lifestyle—but free in terms of time and choices. Many of the best small practitioners, the ones who help people on a daily basis, are penurious or nearly so. But they can set their own hours, play tennis, work at night, and choose which sorts of cases to pursue. To many, the lifestyle is worth more than money.

A professor of social work once pointed out that lawyers and law students are the angry, argumentative sort. Lawyers supposedly die younger, he said, because of all that anger. In my opinion, more lawyers die young because they work for others and follow their rules than because of anger. All the more reason to take charge of your life and open your own law practice.

For those men and women who want to strike out on their own, a small practice offers the most flexibility. The lawyer creates the style of the office. Clients can be treated more humanely. Offices can be more comfortable, more amenable to children, and more open to the public. Solo practitioners and small partnerships can set their own hours and choose their own areas of interest. Most importantly, they are their own bosses, making their own mistakes and winning their own cases. And for the solo practitioner, credit always goes where credit is due—which often has particular appeal to women and minorities.

For many, the small practice is both the riskiest and the most creative way to practice law. This book offers advice to those daring enough to hang up a shingle. The advice is practical as well as philosophical. How can a beginner start a business on a shoestring? Which legal fields should a fledgling small practitioner pursue? How can he or she make money, stay happy, and help others? Is being the good lawyer/good citizen practical or even possible in today's cutthroat society? This manual provides help in answering these questions and shows that the answer to the last question is "yes"—the lawyer who wants to help society become better and stronger has chosen the right profession.

1

Early Decisions

Let's face it, there's no way law school teaches anyone to work as a small practice lawyer—or any other type of lawyer, for that matter. But because law school is there (like Mount Everest), the best way to approach it is to evaluate how law school can help you.

The Relevance of Law School

The first step toward becoming any kind of lawyer is education—which involves a lot of reading and a fair amount of humiliation. School is generally the most painful part of the lawyer's journey and serves as a trial by fire to smoke out those who don't have the heart or stomach to practice law. Most law school classes require students to read 25 pages of case law per night and understand the contents, so the work is intense.

After graduation, the study is less intense, but legal education does not stop after law school. There's the bar review, and if you do happen to pass the bar, the annual doses of continuing legal education courses still remain.

Law school itself does not teach anyone how to run a law practice. It does not teach anyone how to work for a law firm, or become a good government lawyer, or work as in-house counsel. Law school teaches the law: the basics about contracts and real estate closings and the difference between federal law and state law.

> **Smart Tip**
> Law school doesn't prepare you for starting your own practice. Use internships and summer jobs to learn the fundamentals of running an office. Use law school to learn how to do legal research and hone your computer skills.

But law school teaches more than the analysis of cases. One of law school's most salient lessons, for example, is how to withstand ridicule. Law school and the legal professional can be tough. Some law professors enjoy humiliating their students, just as some judges enjoy humiliating the lawyers who appear before them. Lawyers must be able to withstand both and walk out smiling. (The general rule on looking ridiculous in class or dimwitted in court is to allow yourself 24 hours of grieving, but no more). In this way, law school teaches a necessary skill.

Research is another valuable tool acquired in law school: how to find cases in the books and online, how to find statutes, and how to read and interpret them. The law

> **The Whole Truth**
>
> Law school teaches you how to handle defeat and move forward. Time spent mourning a loss in court is time lost on the next case. Losses teach valuable lessons. Always move forward.

librarians teach this as much as professors do. Without this skill, no lawyer could perform the work required, even if he or she had an army of paralegals or student soldiers scouring the library and scanning web sites for pertinent cases. Armies may become lazy and refuse to perform for a general who does not understand basic tactics. Research skills are the basic reconnaissance tactics that every law student must master.

> **Smart Tip**
> During law school, concentrate on learning legal research, both from books and on the internet. After law school, avoid depending on paralegals or clerks. Always find the relevant statutes and case law yourself.

The law school experience may also reveal what type of practitioner you wish to become, whether money is a critical factor in your career plans or working with people is your main goal. And you may learn as much by what's omitted as by what's there. When I attended the University of South Carolina, its main goal was to prepare lawyers in corporate law, tax law, and commercial contracts. There was very little training in criminal defense or family law—and none on social policy or aid programs such as Social Security. Yet the latter were all areas that interested me, eventually. Lack of course work did not affect my goals.

In South Carolina a law student decides to become a plaintiff's attorney, representing individuals, or a defendant's attorney, representing the government, insurance companies, and corporations. There is a wide difference between the two types of attorneys—in personality, style, and legal emphasis. Plaintiffs' attorneys must be gambling, scheming strategists who give their clients confidence, especially on those occasions when the lawyers themselves are taking a gamble. They look to individuals and small companies for their support and client base. And they practice casual Tuesdays, Wednesdays, and Thursdays—or any day when they don't have to appear in court.

Defendant attorneys may tend to be more conservative, more corporate, because of their client base, which is frequently larger companies and institutions. These attorneys, both male and female, wear suits much of the time.

Grades, personalities, and (especially) connections determine which role lawyers *can* play out in the "real world." Personalities also often make a difference in career choice. Those law students who don't want to do corporate work can try to work for the government. Jobs with the state can be fun, and the hours are regular. Plaintiff attorneys can join a smaller firm, with

> **Smart Tip**
> Decide which type of lawyer you want to become while at law school. Do you want to be a criminal defender or a policy enforcer? Government lawyer or advocate in the private sector? Think of what you hope to accomplish, what you want.

> **The Whole Truth**
> Law school exacerbates tension and controversy among the students because exams are graded on a curve, which pits students against each other.

four or five attorneys, a couple of secretaries, and a colorful boss—as I did for a while. Or they can immediately set out on their own or with a partner. Hang up a shingle, plunge forward, and pray.

Law school can be tough, and it's extremely competitive. In my first semester, I watched my fellow students drop out like water from a sieve. Students seated all around me decided to leave. "I'm a math major," one woman rationalized. "I don't need this [expletive deleted]." Others declared that the professors drove them insane, that they could already get a high-paying job and so who needed this, or that they missed their families back home. My main thought following the first semester was "it's either them [the law professors] or me, and it isn't going to be me!"

No one who decided to stay stopped to think about the toll law school would exact from their relationships: law students have been known to experience an 80 percent divorce/breakup rate before the three years were over.

In the end, of course, I got through and with my marriage intact. I became a plaintiffs' attorney—and eventually a solo practitioner. Working as a solo practitioner suits my personality. It enables me to enjoy a lot of one-on-one contact with my clients. I feel as though I'm fighting against the big dogs and making a difference. I wear what I want and set my own hours. These advantages more than make up for the uncertainty of my income.

> **The Whole Truth**
> Law school is tough on relationships. Don't expect your family to understand what you're going through.

Having the Right Stuff to Go Solo

The practice of law provides so many opportunities that it is imperative for the recent law school graduate, or any lawyer contemplating a career change, to sit down and plan what he or she wants to accomplish in life. Tax reform? Social Security reform? A comfortable living? Another important question is what you like to do. Do you enjoy dealing with people and their problems on a daily basis? If the answer is "no," you should stop right here and consider working for the government, a company, or a larger law firm, because opening a solo or small practice is not the right path.

Another issue to consider is whether a steady paycheck is important. Continuous cash flow is not always an option for the solo practitioner. Income acts like a roller coaster for the solo. Sometimes it's way, way up, and sometimes it's down.

The practice of law is fueled by deadlines that cannot be ignored. Lawyers who are not self-motivated, who need to work under the switch or under the continuous direction of others should not choose solo practice. Solo work requires self discipline. A-type personalities can work for themselves; you know who you are already. For the laid-back type, a partnership would be the better choice, especially if the partner has a strong work and management ethic. This does not mean that you have to build a legal sweatshop. Partners must like each other. The goal is to create a situation in which you want to work and where you feel confident the work will get done.

Smart Tip

If you don't enjoy listening to people and their personal problems, don't go into solo practice. Solo attorneys have precious few buffers between themselves and their clients.

The Rules

Not everyone should yell "Trash the system!" and hang out a shingle. There are certain rules to this game. Here are mine:

- Be able to work on your own. This means having the creativity and the foresight to set goals without a boss following your every move.
- Have a secondary source of income if there are children in your household.
- Possess a strong desire to help people.
- Have the ability to listen and empathize.

Working on Your Own

Solo and small practitioners must be able to set their own goals and follow through with them. They are not the sort of people who enjoy working for a boss. In fact, they gain more satisfaction from creating their own rules and making their own mistakes. Solos must have the drive and the self-motivation to carry through with a work plan even when the movie theater or the golf course calls their names. As with any small business, the threat of imminent starvation usually acts as a strong motivator to get the work done on time.

Money

Have a secondary source of income available. My husband teaches at the University of South Carolina. Unlike me, he has a steady paycheck. Most, if not all, of my acquaintances who run solo practices are married to spouses who hold steady jobs. When children are involved, this is necessary. I can picture a single man or woman without children starting a solo law practice and being able to survive through lean times of the year. Single men and women can make popcorn for dinner or may not need large wardrobes. Children are what make the difference in solo practice, and in just about everything else. Having children means that you must have money—a lot of money. Solo practitioners cannot count on making a lot of money. It is not a sure thing for them. For this reason, their partners should be steady earners if they intend to have children.

A Strong Desire to Help People

Solo practitioners must enjoy their clients—a group of people with major, heartbreaking problems. These clients may be physically unwell or emotionally (psychologically) stressed. They might be both sick and crazy because they're going through a divorce. Some are addicted to alcohol or drugs. This one might have been injured in a car wreck. That one's sister might have died and left him with two small children to raise. The worst ones are the recent terminations—those who have been fired from their jobs after 25 years of dedicated work. All of them need someone to talk to, and that someone is the solo practitioner. The lawyer who is uncomfortable with this sort of personal interaction should not become a solo practitioner. Ask yourself: Do you normally have a box of tissues on your desk? Do you think that's a silly suggestion? The solo practitioner needs to have tissues handy, both for his clients and himself.

The Ability to Listen and Empathize

Potential clients all have stories to tell. Everyone in the world has a story to tell, but potential clients need to tell their stories in detail. Clients are in trouble because of the details, and they need someone to listen hard—not someone who is thinking about next weekend's football game. One of the arts of practicing law is perceiving and remembering every part of the story: who takes the child to day care in the morning, whether or not the secretary in the front office made a higher salary than the file clerk in the back office, who was having sex with whom and at what time, whether anyone witnessed the conversation, or how much is recorded in writing. Lawyers who are not interested in the lurid details of other people's lives should not become solo practitioners.

The solo practitioner must do more than listen; she must be able to delve into the clients' personal stories. What is it like to have a son who is psychotic? Why must the alcoholic drink himself to death, all the while denying that he has a problem? How can these people be put at ease and induced to tell the complete truth?

A Force for Change

Attorneys overall need to forge a better relationship with the public. One among the many popular lawyer jokes is:

"What's the difference between a lawyer and a catfish?"
"One's a bottom-dwelling scum sucker. The other is a fish."

The truth is that practicing law, especially at the solo level, is a helping, caring profession. Legal clients have terrible, life-shattering problems. People consult lawyers for help in navigating the legal system, but they also consult lawyers for advice. The lawyer's status as a professional gives him the power to make suggestions and have them heard. He can also do a lot of important work toward changing the legal system for the better by winning cases that give people more rights and lobbying for changes in the law. These possibilities give lawyers a considerable amount of power. They should seize this power and use it to change the profession for the better.

A passion for change can be especially important to solo lawyers. A sole practitioner can create something beautiful. Lawyers should ask what they want to achieve. If their only goal is to make money, they should find a job working for someone else because the average employee accumulates wealth much more easily than the creator of a solo practice. If, instead, they want to build a law office where clients feel comfortable and helped, then running a solo practice is an definite option.

Solos are in a good position to make changes in the legal world because they make the rules for their own work space. The thoughtful solo can instigate a million and one small changes in the way things are done at the courthouse, in jails, or in the world of employment. They're the ones on the front lines, the ones who, via their clients, can see the problems.

The first area that a solo can change is her own office. The office becomes ground zero for making things work more effectively. What setting makes clients feel more at ease? Which hours are the best hours for reading new cases? Which software works best at keeping the money in order? Is a secretary necessary?

Lawyers by their actions can change their clients' lives in big ways. Obtaining Social Security disability money for a client who really needs it can keep him off the street and provide his family with security. Clients consult lawyers for serious advice. One of my clients told me that a remark I made to her and her husband kept their marriage from breaking up. Lawyers can convince clients not to sue as well as to go ahead and assert their rights. In most cases, the lawyer informs the client of his rights, which can change the client's attitude. Lawyers assist clients in making important decisions. Practicing law as a solo is all about becoming involved with people and their lives.

Lawyers can work to change the laws, which they understand better than most, so that everyone benefits. They can lobby for change, both at the federal and the state levels.

> **Smart Tip**
> As a solo practitioner, use your free time (or create free time) to lobby for change.

The Trial Lawyers' Association does it, and they have a lot of clout. Solos, who do not always agree with this group, can lobby for change in their specific areas of practice. Which laws need to be changed? If Social Security disability claims take too long to process, find out why. If guardians wield too much power in family court, see how they can be harnessed and controlled.

Solos generally represent the guy in the street. If practicing solos see flaws in the system, it's likely that much of the public sees these flaws. Call the newspapers. Stir up some dust. Maybe there are hundreds, or even thousands, of voters who agree with you. Gathering a crowd of supporters is the best way to influence legislators.

Politicking aside, many solo practitioners set more personal goals: aiding the hearing impaired, assisting women with their divorces, assuring fathers of equity in custody cases, or bringing Spanish-speaking clients through the maze of workers' compensation information. Helping all sorts of clients navigate the legal system without feeling intimidated is a possibility for every lawyer

Solo practitioners—the first line of defense that many people see when they land themselves in serious, mind-boggling trouble—are perfectly placed to help lawyers improve their public reputation simply by doing their jobs well. Landed in jail? Brother cheated you out of inheritance money? Wrecked the neighbor's car? Who you gonna call? In the United States, at least, the answer is simple: the neighborhood attorney.

Partnerships

Now that you've had a chance to look at solo practice, it's time to consider whether a small partnership would be a better alternative for you. Do you have the right mental state for running a solo lawyer office? Are you up to running what is in effect a small business all on your own? Lawyers in small partnerships deal with many of the same problems and same people as solo practitioners, but they don't have to go it alone and they don't necessarily have to be self-starters. If you want many of the benefits of your own practice without some of the obvious drawbacks, perhaps a partnership would work better for you.

The advantages of having a partner are many. You have support, companionship, and a readily available second opinion. You can take vacations without returning to face a towering load of mail and phone messages. Serious illness or family catastrophe is not so

Smart Tip

Form partnerships with the possibility of breakup in mind. Decide how cases would be divided if the partnership breaks up. How would assets be divided? How would clients be informed, and what kind of choices would clients be given?

worrying because there is another lawyer around who knows the filing system and the computer layout. Indeed, small mishaps and illnesses are not such a problem. You have a backup.

Partners can profit from each other's reputations and activities. If one partner runs for the state legislature, both benefit from the free advertising accompanying the campaign, win or lose. One partner might have time for a city judgeship, as long as the other partner agrees to handle the added burden of the caseload.

The danger comes if one partner begins to resent the other for any reason, including an uneven caseload, an uneven distribution of profits, or simply insufficient income. Partnership agreements need to be written with the possibility of breakup in mind. If one partner decides to leave the practice, can she take clients with her? Will the clients be given the opportunity to decide whether to leave the practice? Which office furniture belongs to whom? Will the building have to be sold or does it belong to one of the partners?

If one of the partners has more money to put into the practice at the beginning, the decision could be made to have that partner purchase the building or office condominium, with the incorporated partnership renting the space from him. The one partner's seed money could be used as a down payment on the property. This eliminates problems that may occur because of arguments over the building. The partner who owns the building will decide if and when to sell the property, and that partner gets to stay in the building if the partnership breaks up.

When one partner is much older or more experienced than the other, the formation of an uneven partnership is common. A 60–40 partnership might be appropriate when one of the partners has less experience than the other. Once all office expenses have been paid, the profits from the law office are divided 60–40 at the end of the month.

Depending on the level of trust between partners and the personalities of the attorneys, it might be wise to have one partner make all business decisions on office expenses. If one of the partners wants to use office money for an expensive item, such as to attend a law course in Hawaii, it would, however, be good to give the other partner the opportunity to nix such a plan.

> **Smart Tip**
> Have all partners sign a contract at the beginning of the partnership. Get advice from an attorney and an accountant who know about partnerships and incorporations.

At any rate, a decision needs to be made at the beginning as to how office finances will be handled. Who pays the office staff and decides how much the partners will divide at the end of the month? Must checks be signed by both partners? Is one partner to be given the unenviable task of going over the books each month? Will the office use Quicken, or some other program, to keep track of finances?

The dynamics of a partnership depend on the personalities of the attorneys involved. Friends from law school might quickly become enemies under the pressures of running a law office. Perfect strangers could work in perfect harmony. This is why partnerships must be planned with their dissolution in mind. Have everyone sign a contract at the beginning.

Dispelling Myths about Lawyers: Dead Snakes and Evildoers

My favorite joke about lawyers goes like this:

"What is the difference between a dead ratttlesnake in the middle of the road and a dead lawyer in the middle of the road?"

Answer:

"There are skid marks in front of the snake."

The problem with dealing with an image like this is that it rings so true for so many lawyers. Many plaintiffs' attorneys, defendants' attorneys, corporate practitioners, and government counsel see themselves as hired guns placed in the courtroom to win at all costs. Steamrolling over everyone (and costing their clients a bundle of money), they often win high accolades from their employers and their clients, none of whom are considering the big picture.

But even worse for the reputation of the profession, many lawyers wind up on the front page of the newspaper or as the lead story on local TV for actions far less savory. Attorneys who wish to follow the straight and narrow need to be aware of traps and temptations. Although the following rules may seem obvious, they illustrate the pitfalls that land some lawyers in trouble and strip others of their licenses

Don't Steal the Clients' Money

Whether they are dealing with real estate transactions or Social Security disability, attorneys have access to clients' money and intimate knowledge of their financial situations. Many small firms deal with real estate closings because the paperwork is consistent and most of the work can be handled by a paralegal. This means that at some point, the attorney will have large amounts of money in escrow: down payments, mortgage pay-offs, money for title insurance, and tax prepayments. Multiply these dollar amounts by two or three houses, and the temptation is clear. Money placed in escrow belongs to the clients, but the attorney is the one with the power to write those checks.

A golden rule of practicing law is to regard the clients' money as sacred. This may seem childishly fundamental, but it is an area that gets attorneys into more trouble than any other. Money in escrow usually has an established purpose, such as paying child support or paying for a house. This money is easier to regard as sacred because it's easier to trace. The effects of misusing and embezzling escrow money may be immediately apparent to the client.

> **Bright Idea**
> Always keep the client's money separate from your own. Use escrow accounts and an accounting system such as Quicken that allows you to tag the clients' money and create a list of income and expenses for each client.

What's more difficult is to bill clients with complete honesty. Padding bills may be encouraged at the larger law firms, but small practices need to avoid that practice. Keeping accurate records of the work done is the best way to bill the client with honesty. While writing bills, pretend that the client is looking over your shoulder. If a telephone call from a client lasts for 15 minutes, billing for 30 minutes would be tricky to justify; the client might remember how long the phone call lasted. If you use a "canned" brief to write a divorce complaint, and it took 30 minutes to compose, don't charge for two hours! . Pretend that the client is watching. Pretend that you are writing a bill for yourself. Remember how *you* felt the last time your car mechanic overcharged for an oil change. Attorneys are helping professionals, and they need to set the standard for integrity, not become fodder for cocktail party humor.

Don't Misuse Your Power

Lawyers are expensive, and many times in family law situations, for example, one side is lawyered up, while the other side is acting *pro se* (representing himself, without a lawyer). It would be tempting to take advantage of this situation and avoid serving the unrepresented party with necessary paperwork, for example, or talk him into signing a lopsided settlement agreement, one leaning your client's way. Most of the time, the court system ensures that parties acting *pro se* get served properly. The lopsided settlement agreement becomes mighty tempting, however, when the opposing party cannot afford a lawyer or just wants to rid himself of the case as quickly as possible. "Want this divorce to be over quickly? Just sign here. You won't even need to come to court." It's tempting, but wrong.

> **Smart Tip**
> Avoid taking advantage of pro se opponents. Suggest they call legal services. Do not, however, give advice to these litigants.

There are some simple ways to avoid snaring the unrepresented party.

- Make sure the *pro se* party understands you do not represent her. Many lay people are under the false impression that a divorce can be handled by one attorney, who somehow represents both parties. Let the *pro se* party know in writing that you do not represent her and that you are acting in the best interests of your client only.
- Encourage the unrepresented party to obtain a lawyer. This should be done often and with sincerity. Having two lawyers on a divorce case often causes the case to proceed more smoothly anyway.
- When presenting the unrepresented party with a settlement agreement, ask her *again* to retain a lawyer to read it over. Do not say "let your accountant read this" or "your recently-divorced neighbor should give his opinion." Specify that she needs a lawyer. Friends and neighbors are usually full of half-baked advice about what should happen in divorce court, and they are very bad counselors.

Stick to the Truth

Lawyers should no more lie about a client's situation than doctors should. First of all, be completely honest with your clients. Any lawyer who promises a client that he will win before a particular judge or jury is, in effect, lying. Appearing before a judge or jury is like tossing a coin. Always. No one can predict the outcome with any accuracy, other than saying "You have a 50/50 chance of winning."

More reprehensible than lying to a client is misrepresenting facts in open court. If your client has a drug problem, for example, bring this to light. Failure to do so may result in the endangerment of children, the death of innocent drivers, and a burden on the community in general.

Smart Tip
Avoid any temptation to mislead your client or the court. Tell the whole truth and be a stickler about bringing problems out into the open, especially when they involve the care of children.

A trick sometimes used by corporate counsel is the alteration or destruction of relevant documents: journals, e-mail, business records, or financial statements. The small office lawyer, who will become aware of this practice very early on in his career, should not fall into the same trap. Cases can often be won or lost on paperwork. Memoranda are more reliable than people's memories. Juries like to see what was written down at the time of the conflict. In employment cases, lists showing salaries often speak volumes, which is why companies often prefer to keep such lists secret. In a quest for truth, it would be unjust to alter or destroy the evidence that documents what happened. Practitioners can use documents to gauge the worth of a case. Use documents wisely. Don't abuse them.

Avoid Conflicts of Interest

Opportunities for conflicts of interest are numerous and dangerous. Sexual indiscretions has led many attorneys astray. Other conflicts are less obvious: your own or your spouse's competing financial interests or competing legal interests are not always so obvious but no less dangerous.

Sex with a client or even relatives of a client is crossing a line. Don't do it, even after the case is over! Besides ensuring a fast trip to the grievance commission of the bar, a sexual relationship can mess up a case and eliminate the chance of future referrals from that client. Before accepting a case, make an initial choice between a relationship and representation, and stick with that choice.

Another way to avoid conflicts is to refuse to represent a client simultaneously on two different matters. Do not agree to represent a client on a divorce matter while a criminal case is pending. You can represent a client on two different matters, but not at the same time. Problems on one case could affect the attorney-client relationship on the other case, which creates a conflict.

An obvious conflict occurs when an attorney decides to sue a person, company, or government agency with which he has an existing relationship. My husband works at the university, for example, so I would not sue the university. If I served as a board member, I would avoid suing that company. If I had a friendship with Sue Ellen, I would decline to sue her in family court. The basic question to ask is, "Would my work as an attorney be affected by my relationship with that entity?" If personal, monetary, or convivial interests would lessen the vigor with which I pursued the case, then I should decide against bringing that lawsuit. Be honest with yourself. Farm it out.

Conflicts of Interest

To avoid conflicts of interest:
- Never engage in romance or friendship with a client.
- Do not represent clients on more than one matter at a time.
- Say "no" to representing witnesses in legal matters.
- Avoid representing businesses in which you or your spouse has a financial interest.
- Avoid suing entities in which you or your spouse has a financial interest.

Choosing the Right Areas of Practice

It has always seemed strange to me when solo practitioners advertise that they have "a general practice" or that they perform "all types of litigation." With a partnership of two or three attorneys, it might be possible to keep up with several areas of the law, but for a solo, this is nearly impossible. Staying up-to-date on a particular area of the law, such as divorce, employment law, or criminal defense, involves being proactive. Reading the current case law and new statutes, talking with other lawyers practicing in the same area, doing research, and appearing in court with those cases on a regular basis are all necessary components of remaining competent in a particular area. I believe that one lawyer—with a life outside the office—can stay competent in three or four areas of the law, but no more. One of those areas might be criminal defense, which covers a lot of territory. Another area might be employment law, which requires experience before judges (liberal, conservative, and Machiavellian) because reading cases and statutes cannot communicate the complete picture.

The best way to gain experience in a particular area of law is by working beside another attorney—a dinosaur of a mentor—because those experienced guys and gals know all the ropes. When a young lawyer can absorb the experience of a dinosaur and put fresh eyes on the situation, the learning experience is beautiful. I learned employment law and procedure by sitting beside an experienced employment attorney in the courtroom and assisting. Sitting second chair is invaluable experience for a new lawyer. Another lawyer taught me how to write the pleadings.

In the area of family law, which is more complex than it appears, I had the help of another attorney friend. His pleadings were not always the best, but he knew family law. He kept up with the statutes and the case law. He could answer almost any question about family law and criminal domestic violence, and if he didn't know the answer, he knew where to find it.

> **Bright Idea**
> Choose three or four areas of law to practice. Don't be a "general practitioner." Mentors can help narrow the choices. Listen to your heart and your pocketbook when choosing areas in which to practice.

Being a mentor is not easy. But it is vital to the profession. Others helped me. I'll help others—and you will, too, down the line.

When deciding on which three or four areas of practice you want to focus on, ask the following questions:

1. What does the public need and want from a lawyer in your geographic area?
2. Do you wish to practice mainly in court or out of court?

3. Do you wish to deal with alleged criminals?
4. Which areas of the law do you feel passionate about?
5. Which areas of the law can your mentors teach you?
6. Which areas of the law are easiest to deal with?
7. Which areas will make you the most amount of money with the least hassle?
8. Which areas of law will stay in demand in your area for a long period of time, regardless of fashion, legislation, or the vagaries of human rights? Possible choices here include family law, personal injury, and criminal defense.

First Choice: The Passion

Because a lawyer can choose three or four areas, one area can be whatever interests him. More often than not, this area is *not* a money-maker. My areas of legal passion are employment law and copyright law. Copyright questions are so few and far between that it only qualifies as one-twelfth of an area of practice. There is a larger demand for employment law, but in South Carolina the rights of the employee are unpopular. That's what makes it fun. It is my one legal passion. It keeps me going.

> **The Whole Truth**
> Choose at least one area of law that you care about passionately, or you will be snoring at your desk. You need to be interested in your work. Solos do not have office politics to keep them awake!

On the downside, employment cases are lengthy and expensive. They involve a lot of discovery and immense cooperation from the plaintiff. Lawyers should not attempt these cases without a large retainer fee, money for costs paid up front, and some concrete proof that the discrimination or nonpayment of wages actually occurred. All in all, I would not recommend that any new lawyer take up employment law without a mentor close by. Advising someone to do this would be criminal. Those who feel a passion for this kind of work know who they are and will find themselves a mentor to work with. The rest should find something else to do.

Second Choice: The Old Standard

The practitioner's second area of law should be an old standard, such as family law or criminal defense, that will survive the hurricane season and just about anything else. Most likely there will always be divorces, and there will always be criminals, and slip-and-falls. Auto accidents, insurance defense, tax law, and probate are other possibilities. Choose an area that someone close by can teach you. I chose family law because it was an old standard and because I had someone handy to teach me the ropes.

Family law allows the practitioner to earn a steady income and charge by the hour. The trick is enticing the clients to walk through the door. This is an area of the law, like criminal defense, that is rife with competition. The successful family practitioner must be able to offer something different—such as the reputation of being hard-nosed, or offering personal service, or lower hourly rates. I offer lower rates and personal service.

> **Smart Tip**
> Choose one area of law that will always exist. Bankruptcy will probably always be around and so will divorces.

Criminal defense was never an option because I could not get past the first step, which was representing clients accused of driving under the influence. On the other hand, these clients often have jobs to protect, and they are willing to pay hefty retainer fees up front. And, the American judicial system would not work without good criminal defense. It just wasn't for me.

Third Choice: Lucrative Relaxation

The third choice is the relaxing choice: an area of law that is both simple and lucrative. One of my acquaintances, Andrea, chose bankruptcy, which is governed by paperwork and a series of steps dictated by statutory law. She likes doing the math and helping people. She has friends in bankruptcy court. Bankruptcy law makes her happy.

My relaxing area is Social Security disability: helping clients obtain benefits. I enjoy the strict parameters and the politics. Social Security practice has its own rules that make my life easier: precise retainer agreements, its own special forms, a strict regimen for receiving payment, and deadlines for filing responses and pleadings. I don't have to worry about wrangling money from the client up front. My fee comes out of the benefits, if and when we win. That erases a huge burden. Social Security clients tend to be grateful and cooperative. Second, the cases are winnable. I can see a clear path to obtaining the benefits. If the client cooperates and has medical proof of disability, I can usually win the administrative hearing. Third, the work is straightforward and does not involve an attorney on the other side until you reach the federal court level. I am proving disability to a federal agency, with no opposing lawyer contesting my facts.

In addition, Social Security offers an opportunity for activism. This is our social welfare system. The Social Security practitioner comes to realize that without this program, our country would be in a sorry state. Social Security disability benefits are often the last safety net for the families of working adults who lose their jobs through illness. When a working adult dies, her dependents can collect benefits. Because Medicaid eligibility is tied in with Social Security disability, becoming eligible often means that the Social Security recipient can see a doctor when he could not before.

In the beginning, choosing one's areas of practice often involves more luck than choice. The attorney who happens to practice next door becomes a valuable mentor. Her areas of practice become your areas of practice. Whatever walks in off the street may influence your choice. If client Carmen has an interesting case, it might become your passion and your favorite area of practice. You win Carmen's case, you make a lot of money, and a specialty is born. Personal interests and foci before law school oftentimes shape which area of the law you tackle. A local issue or environmental disaster catches your fancy. You get a client, you do some research, and you're off.

As the small practice lawyer matures in the profession, experience plays more of a role in that choice. Successes and failures. Terrible judges. Good settlements that send the clients home happy. Sometimes specialties dry up because of new legislation or case law that limits the amount the client can recover. Luckily, areas of practice can be discarded and replaced. In the legal world, there's always something new to learn, always something happening. The beauty of practicing alone is that the solo practitioner is always free to reinvent himself or herself. And, with a few limitations, this is also true of lawyers in small partnerships.

2

Your Office

For those who plunge into a solo or small partnership practice, the location of the first office and the kind of law practiced by the first neighbors do a lot to shape the direction of a career. For instance, I started out my solo law practice by renting office space from three attorneys who taught me some legal tricks and steered me toward employment law.

This office was very close to the federal courthouse, which made it convenient to file employment discrimination cases. I could have chosen federal criminal defense or securities and exchange law, of course, but none of my landlords were doing those things. As my practice matured, my client base shifted to family law and Social Security, but I never lost touch with employment law.

Style of the Office: Projecting an Image

Your office may occasionally become your second home during times of work crisis, and for that reason it should look and feel good to you. Your office also has to be right for your clients—to make them comfortable. You will spend a lot of time in your office, and it should reflect your personality and the image you want to present to clients.

My own office is filled with secondhand wooden furniture, antiques whenever possible, and photographs. Many are photographs of my family; some are photographs a friend took in India. The most prized picture is a crayon drawing of fish by my daughter.

The best way to furnish the basics of a new office is with secondhand furniture found in newspaper classifieds. After that, add as many or as few personal touches as you feel comfortable with. Just remember, you'll be spending a lot of time here. Don't be too cheap.

> **The Whole Truth**
>
> The location of your first office, the attorneys who practice near you or in the same building, and your proximity to certain courthouses all have a strong impact on the type of law you end up practicing. Look for possible mentors among your neighbors.

> **Smart Tip**
>
> Make sure that your building and your office say something about your personality. Don't be afraid to decorate with photographs of your family or prized memorabilia. Clients appreciate the personal touches that teach them about your family and your history.

Accessibility

Accessiblity can be a major selling point, particularly for a solo attorney, and it can be a pain. Clients like you to be available. But sometimes availability means it's hard to get work done at the office—which after all is part of the point of an office. You'll need to decide how willing you are to tolerate walk-ins, people who come in off the street. Accessible doesn't have to mean availability to everyone all the time.

Clients like to be able to talk directly to attorneys, with as few intermediaries as possible. That certainly appeals greatly to my clients. I don't have a secretary. I answer my own phone. This may mean that the client has to leave a message, but he can be sure that I will be listening to those messages and returning the calls myself. Many clients hire me because they appreciate this personal service and close attention.

The style of my office reflects this immediacy. When clients walk in they can usually see me sitting in my office or reception area. They can see I'm not hiding out, chatting with colleagues or wasting clients' time. Clients have said that when a particular attorney kept them waiting for no good reason, they simply walked out and hired a different attorney. Clients are willing to wait—if they can see that you are dealing with another client or talking on the phone with a judge. Clients respect attorneys who respect the clients' time.

> **Smart Tip**
> Decide on a strategy to deal with walk-ins. Will you make time to see them right away or always ask them to make an appointment, even if you're doing paperwork? How should walk-ins off the street be treated differently from walk-in clients who just happen to be in the neighborhood?

Some attorneys thrive on walk-in clients. They might handle auto accidents and have a receptionist ready to greet potential clients from the neighborhood. Others, like me, do not. But everyone has to decide on a policy to deal with them. If I'm not seeing another client or preparing for a hearing, I do tend to talk with potential clients at least for a few minutes. Once a person has retained me, I discourage them from walking in unannounced, however, unless it's to drop off paperwork or inform me of an emergency situation.

Accessibility, for better or worse, includes accessibility to children. The solo practitioner must have safe toys and a play space available for children because clients often bring children with them, whether you want them to or not. The space doesn't have to be large, and the supply of toys doesn't have to be huge. (A video room would be ideal.) But you need a few toys and magazines to keep kids of all ages occupied and out of earshot when talking to parents. Do not permit a child of any age to sit in your office while a parent is ranting and raving about the other.

Location, Location, Location

The lawyer who is seeing clients face-to-face should not run a law office at home. Of course, there are exceptions to this rule; some lawyers do manage to work at home. An attorney who only does appellate work—interacting with other lawyers and records on appeal and filing paperwork—does not need a downtown office with a sign out front. Usually, however, the home/office doesn't work for solo practitioners.

Clients are sometimes dangerous. They may be upset, under incredible pressure, they may threaten to kill other people and sometimes themselves. They may suffer from diseases such as hepatitis C and AIDS or are high on drugs. For these reasons, it is imprudent and uncomfortable to run a law office at home, especially around children or partners. In addition, there is the mental health of the lawyer to consider. Home is a haven and a getaway after dealing with upset clients. Home should be kept at a distance from the office, both mentally and physically.

Locate your office downtown, near courthouses and other attorneys, even if the location is not ideal. Make sure you have plenty of free parking.

A location that's easy to get to and close to residential areas is also good, although it's limiting to locate in a purely residential area. You're probably only able to serve that particular community. This is not advisable unless you're a tax attorney. To reach a wider variety of clients, it's better to locate downtown, even if in many cities this is not always the safest place to work.

In addition, courts, both local and federal, are usually downtown. Proximity to the various courts is a big plus. It's convenient and a huge time saver. There's a reason so many law offices circle the courthouses.

The number of law offices near the courts means it's difficult to get a well-located office away from other lawyers. That's a problem for some lawyers. They argue that being close to other attorneys isn't a good idea, but others, like me, disagree. Proximity to other lawyers, especially other small practitioners, can generate referrals, provide mentors, and give you access to people who understand your work and its problems and pleasures.

My office is not in a safe part of town. The building, however, is in a great location. It's close to other attorneys. The main artery into Columbia—Interstate 26—passes into the city one block from my office, which makes giving directions to people easy. I'm within walking distance of a couple of residential neighborhoods, four restaurants, and two gas stations. All of this is good for business. There are parks within few blocks for quick exercise.

With regard to courthouses, my office location is ideal. The new federal district courthouse is right across the street. Social Security hearings are held five blocks away; I could walk if I had to. Bankruptcy court is within walking distance, and the county courthouse is a short drive away. I can even walk to the post office if the weather is fine.

That's a perfect location. The size of your city will determine if you can get so many positive factors in one place. Just balance what matters most to you and what you can do with the money available.

Getting Started

After finding a suitable office, the solo practitioner or new partnership has a few tasks that need immediate attention. These are neither complicated nor formidable for someone who has graduated from law school and passed the bar exam. But they are necessary—both to protect you and to protect your clients.

Business License

A law practice is a business, so your first task is to apply for a business license according to your local state laws. This may require a yearly renewal around tax time, and the fees can be variable. The fee for a business license in South Carolina, for example, is dependent on the previous year's gross income.

Incorporation

Incorporation has become an easy, inexpensive process in many states. Although incorporation cannot shield the attorney from personal liability with regard to his professional errors or negligence, it does help form a barrier, or the illusion of a barrier, between the attorney's work and his personal finances.

Incorporation *never* takes the place of liability insurance. It does help draw the line between actions of the attorney and her associates with regard to legal services and actions of the attorney as a private citizen. In the mind of the public, the attorney and her business are now two separate entities. Incorporation, however, does not shield the attorney from professional liability for all of her actions as an attorney.

Before incorporating as either a professional corporation or a limited liability corporation, every lawyer should check with an accountant regarding the tax consequences. The accountant may advise against incorporation for various reasons.

> **Smart Tip**
> A certified public accountant can advise the solo practitioner or small partnership on whether to incorporate and how to incorporate. An attorney should never incorporate without first receiving some expert advice on the tax consequences. Each attorney's situation will be different.

Liability Insurance

No attorney should practice law without liability insurance. Because of the high premiums, some lawyers practice without insurance. They put their residences in their spouses' names and avoid direct ownership of anything worth suing for. Practicing without liability insurance, however, is a terrible idea. The insurance is there to protect the attorney as well as the clients.

Look to your state bar and your colleagues for advice on which insurance company to choose. Long before anyone considers bringing a lawsuit or a grievance against the

> **Beware!**
> When a problem occurs that might lead to a lawsuit or a grievance against the attorney, report the details to the insurance carrier as soon as possible. Report any problems with disgruntled clients, whether or not the attorney has made an error. Clients have been known to file frivolous lawsuits against attorneys.

practitioner, a good professional liability insurance company offers seminars and newsletters on ethics to help attorneys avoid mistakes. It will also provide counseling and advice if the lawyer falls into difficulty or makes a mistake.

If a heated problem occurs, the good insurance company will advise a lawyer when to offer a settlement in order to avoid being sued. If the lawyer is sued, the insurance company provides a defense attorney. All of this equals peace of mind and a practical advantage that every lawyer needs.

Start out with the smallest coverage available and consider increasing to the next level after practicing for three years. If the insurance company offers a "first dollar defense" option, meaning automatic payment of defense costs (without a deductible) if a frivolous lawsuit is filed against the attorney, take this option.

Report everything to the insurance company. Report any mistake or act of negligence on your part and any client dissatisfaction that could possibly turn into a lawsuit or grievance. Report it the same day it happens or as soon as possible. Many insurance companies protect their clients on a "reporting" basis. This means they won't cover you if a client sues you and you knew about the problem six months before. If you don't make an incident report to the insurance company as soon as you suspect a problem, the insurance won't cover you with regard to that problem.

Reporting should not cause your premiums to increase. What may cause your premiums to increase is the money spent by the insurance company if you *do* get sued or they have to appoint an attorney to defend you. Mere reporting and regular communication with the insurance company are part of the company's daily routine. They should be able to absorb this cost without charging more to their clients.

Many state bars will not allow lawyers to subscribe to their referral services unless they have adequate liability insurance. Don't go into court without it.

Office Equipment and Record-Keeping

Lawyers have to maintain many client files. Every exhibit, pleading, and piece of correspondence needs to be recorded in hard copy, and whenever possible, in computer records. This is necessary to trace the progress of a case for both yourself and the client, to try a case, and to show a judge what has occurred and what has been filed in court. These files need to be maintained and stored for a number of years after the case has ended.

Files

When setting up a filing system for paper files, it's best to go with the cheapest option. Don't use legal file cabinets and legal-sized folders just because they're called "legal." Use letter-sized file cabinets. Four-drawer, legal-sized file cabinets cost about $50 more per cabinet and are three inches wider than letter-sized cabinets. The narrower letter-sized files are easier to handle. The paper costs less. The files cost less. They're easier to store.

Have plenty of room for filing old and new cases. Most state bars require lawyers to keep old files on hand for a minimum of six years. This rule means that you will be required to keep a multitude of old files around, and be able to access them even after you stop practicing law. If an old client files a grievance against you, it's necessary to be able to put your hands on that file immediately. You must have access to the paper file and maybe the computer file containing that case.

> **Smart Tip**
> When a case is over, always write a letter to the client informing him or her that the attorney–client relationship is over. Some clients, relying on the old notion of the family attorney, have been known to assume that they retained the attorney for the client's natural life.

Once a client has been "dismissed," (either the case has ended and you've written the client a letter informing her that the attorney–client relationship no longer exists, or the client has found another attorney), it's necessary to decide which papers in the file to keep. All pleadings and correspondence should go into the closed file. Affidavits and depositions should not be thrown away. Any essential paper evidence provided by the client should be kept available, mainly because the client may come back looking for it.

> **Beware!**
> *Never* hand over the entire file to the client without retaining copies of the important parts (pleadings, correspondence, etc.). The client must always have access to the file, but the attorney must also keep a copy for himself.

Although the client must have complete access to his file at any time, *never* hand a file over to a present client or former client without keeping a copy yourself. The file is the evidence of the work you've done. Let the client examine the file in your office. It's better to keep the original and copy whatever portion of the file the client desires for him to take away.

New cases can be arranged in alphabetical order by the names of the clients. When filing old cases, keep in mind that in the future you may want to discard any cases that are six or more (or some other number of years) old. File the closed cases by number. Keep a card file, in alphabetical order, of the cases. That way you can look up "Jones, Samantha" and see that her case is number 268, closed on May 15, 2004.

Computers and their Programs

Choose the word processing system that is popular in your town. Compatible word processing systems can make the exchange of documents easier. Of course, fashions change. Lawyers in South Carolina, for example, tended to use WordPerfect® for a long time. Now, Microsoft Word® is just as popular.

With the increasing popularity of electronic filing, it is also helpful to have the ability to create PDF files. The most popular program here is Adobe Acrobat®.

Always have two computer systems (computer, monitor, printer, and internet connection) working in case one of them crashes in the middle of a meeting or at the apex of an important brief. Make sure that each case has its own CD, filed alphabetically.

Be sure to have an external drive for further back up. Each night, download all current information onto this external, removable drive. Take the external drive home with you. Back up your work as though your computer could die at any moment. One scanner, to add exhibits to electronic files, and to copy forms, is probably sufficient.

Printers

Don't worry about investing in top-quality laser printers that cost an arm and a leg. Think "ease of operation." Choose a printer model that can handle envelopes without a fuss. Make sure that the ink cartridges are easy to remove and replace. A printer that doubles as a fax or triples as a fax machine and copier is the most economical machine to buy. The Hewlett Packard Officejet® 4215 All-In-One even quadruples as a printer, fax, scanner, and copier. This is an excellent machine to buy because it's easy to use and eliminates the need for a separate fax machine.

Copiers

Even with such a printer, you still need a separate copier. Copiers are important to the office because attorneys copy scores of documents every day. A multi-use printer is simply not efficient enough. See what the other small practitioners are buying. Observe them removing jammed paper and note the level of frustration. If an attorney cannot remove jammed paper without calling the secretary, select another type of copier.

The copier doesn't have to be the fanciest machine on the market. It doesn't have to stand on the floor. It doesn't have to collate (although this feature is a nice addition to the office later on when you're richer). What is important is that the copier is reliable, moderately priced, and capable of handling a stack of 25 pages in the feeder. Copying a 25-page document one page at a time can be a waste of time. Be sure to check the price and availability of the ink cartridge and toner because you're going to be buying a lot. Fortunes have been spent on cartridges and toner.

> **Smart Tip**
> Select cheap printers, telephones, facsimile machines, and internet access. The operative word here is "cheap," which is how the new attorney must think when first hanging up a shingle. Do, however, select two reliable computers, whether they are cheap or expensive.

Telephone Systems and Internet Connections

There is no need for a fancy telephone system in the small law office. Two or three lines will suffice, one for each attorney's incoming calls and one for all incoming faxes. The fax line can double as the internet line, if you still have dial-up service. Oftentimes, for the busy small practitioner, avoiding telephone calls becomes the main objective of the day.

Select the cheapest form of internet access that allows you to have the necessary e-mail accounts and to do online research. Avoid buying an expensive research service, especially one that charges by the minute. Recent case law is available through such free search engines as Findlaw. Find out if your bar association or local law library offers any legal search tools. Use the free search engines, and then move onto book research if there is a law library available.

Law Books

The only legal books necessary in the beginning are a set of state statutes (which must be updated regularly) and the state rules of procedure, both civil and criminal. A set of state statutes is necessary because you must be able to carry the individual books to court. Also, annotated state statutes make an excellent springboard for initiating legal research.

Pay attention to the local rules of procedure enforced by the nearest federal district court. Obtain a copy of these rules and keep it updated. The procedure in federal court is often very different from the procedure in lower courts.

> **Bright Idea**
> Purchase a set of state statutes, and state and federal rule books. These, plus dictionaries, are all the books a beginning small office needs. Later, it could be wise to purchase a specialty book on one or more areas of practice. Patent lawyers will need to have their patent regulations. Social Security regulations are useful to have on hand. There's always a good family law handbook that other attorneys recommend.

Federal statutes are too expensive for a small practitioner to maintain except for some special books related to a more developed practice. Federal statutes are available online. Specialists in such areas as tax law and Social Security can purchase the federal regulations related to those areas by calling the U.S. Printing Office.

Once you have chosen your areas of specialty, it's helpful to purchase "text" books on that subject, perhaps those written by practitioners experienced in your areas of the law. These books provide a starting point for research. They aren't necessary at the beginning, but they make life a lot easier when the time comes to do research before a difficult hearing or trial.

Bank Accounts

Solo practitioners and small partnerships need to open escrow and business accounts in order to keep funds separate. Let the bank know that you need to set up an escrow account for a law office. Attorneys are not allowed to collect interest on most escrow accounts.

Money entrusted to the attorney for the payment of child support or for expenses such as depositions should be placed in escrow rather than co-mingled with the regular business account. For the attorney specializing in real estate closings, an escrow account is very important. Down payments and money for the purchase of property pass directly through escrow and should never linger in an attorney's personal or business account.

Using an easy accounting system such as Quicken® makes the bookkeeping related to banking easier and more accessible at the end of the year. Most small practices need an accountant to handle their tax preparation. Quicken, with its categories, makes it easy to report to the accountant how much was spent on items such as postage, rent, or employees' salaries. Quicken also allows the attorney to ascertain which client paid him money, when, and for

> **Beware!**
> Keep careful account of the funds in your escrow account. Have statements available. Know which client or clients the money belongs to.

what. The Quicken program and a good CPA are two of the small legal practitioners' best friends.

Basic Forms

The small law office needs examples of pleadings; they are vital to the life of the firm. Having mentors who will answer questions and attorneys in your neighborhood and who are willing to share forms will help fulfill this need. Keeping a good library of motions, briefs, financial declarations, subpoenas, verifications, consent orders, final divorce decrees, and complaints of every variety is a necessity, not a choice.

Usually there is little time to contemplate the finer points of a brief. Clarity and precision are what matter. The client, the judge, and especially the judge's clerk should be able to understand what the lawyer has written.

Writing concise pleadings that work is a skill many law schools pretend to teach, but do not. A decent complaint should contain enough detail to frame the situation and enough detail to sustain the causes of action. Law schools may not always teach their students how to write a complaint, the basic building block of a case. Law schools attempt to teach appellate briefs and summary judgment motions, but the motion to compel or the simple rule to show cause is sometimes not included.

Law school professors, who grade on the basis of final written exams, expect students to pepper their law school briefs with clusters of case law. Sometimes this is necessary, especially when a lawyer goes off to work for a defense firm that charges by the hour. A summary judgment motion from an employment defense firm will contain tons of case citations. The plaintiff's attorney, however, is looking for the one or two cases that prove his point. The one Fourth Circuit decision that is on point and says exactly what the plaintiff needs it to say is worth more than the 15 cases that the defense attorney has used to lengthen his motion for summary judgment. The plaintiff's attorney needs that one decision that will win over the judge.

But before answering the juicy motion for summary judgment, the plaintiff's attorney needs to build up a storehouse of basic forms: a summons, complaint for divorce, temporary order, consent order for extension of time to respond, rule to show cause, guardian *ad litem*'s report, witness affidavit, affidavit of attorney's fees, affidavit of service, and a final order. These are the weapons of the divorce attorney. Some of them are available in the rule books; some are not.

> **Smart Tip**
> Maintain a computer file of basic forms such as a summons, different forms of complaints, cover sheets, an acceptance of service, and a subpoena. Beg and borrow examples from other attorneys, and then hone them to suit your practice.

The employment lawyer, practicing in both federal and state courts, employs a different set of weapons. The court has standard discovery responses that must be filed *with* the initial complaint. This sort of knowledge can only be collected through trial and error (which incites the wrath of the federal clerk's office) or by hearing it from another attorney. The latter method is *always* superior. You can share your lack of knowledge with fellow attorneys, but keep it secret from the clerk of court!

4

Frugality

Unless there's a golden pot of money available, the beginning practitioner, solo or partner, needs to think long and hard about whether to hire any employees. Employees are extremely pricey, and they can be problematic. The cost of salary, employer-paid taxes, and health care for one secretary-receptionist can be high enough to drive a new lawyer into the poorhouse. And new lawyers are not the only ones who suffer. An experienced attorney, on his way to retirement, was heard to remark, "It was the secretary's salary that killed me."

Employees

In these days of word processing, answering services, and internet research, the new practitioner definitely *does not* need a paralegal. This is especially true when the attorney is learning how to write the pleadings himself. What might be useful is a receptionist to answer the telephone and take messages when the attorney is out of the office or meeting with clients. Some office buildings offer receptionist services—a person to answer the phone and a place for incoming clients to wait. If the office location is good, the price reasonable, and the rooms for rent are acceptable, the advantages of having a shared receptionist should figure highly in deciding whether to choose this office space.

> **Smart Tip**
> In the beginning, choose to hire a receptionist rather than a more expensive paralegal. If there are two or more attorneys in the building, check out the possibility of sharing a receptionist.

The new lawyer who cannot type, cannot turn on the computer, and absolutely must have her own secretary should proceed cautiously. Once hiring has taken place, employees are difficult to terminate. The firing process takes an emotional toll on everyone involved and could present legal difficulties. Consider hiring someone part time at first, going through a temporary agency. Temporary agencies will place employees in your office for a trial period and switch them with someone else if you, or the secretary, become dissatisfied. The advantage of being able to find the right person through trial and error makes the temporary agency a desirable option. On a legal note, employees working through a temporary service are considered employees of both the law office where they are working and the temporary agency, until the lawyer takes steps to hire that employee.

When employee hours per week are variable, figuring out the state and federal taxes and other costs can be a challenge. If the employee herself is not able to figure the taxes, consider placing this burden on your accountant. Some accounting offices have lesser staff members who handle payroll.

Know the Law

Before searching for a secretary or paralegal, read the laws in your state dealing with employer-employee relations. Become familiar with the federal statutes as well,

> **Smart Tip**
> If you must hire someone yourself, consider using a temporary agency, which gives you the option of trying someone out before deciding to take him on full time.

particularly Title VII (the anti-discrimination laws within U.S. Code 42), the age discrimination laws, and the Americans with Disabilities Act.

Is it necessary in your state to provide a new employee with *written* notice of her hours and wages before offering her the job? When does it become obligatory to provide worker's compensation insurance? Under the Family Medical Leave Act (FMLA), how long must a job be held open for an employee who is on leave caring for a sick relative? Does the FMLA apply to your office? How many employees do you have? Can duly earned wages ever be withheld in your state? Any employer, especially a lawyer, who hires someone without knowing these laws is making a mistake. Professing ignorance of the law is less likely to get a lawyer off the hook than another employer. Even a doctor can argue, "I just didn't understand the law."

One lawyer remarked, "Don't ever hire a woman with small children." That's just plain discriminatory. What about a man with small children? Would he also be frequently unavailable because of the children's illnesses? Any lawyer who decides to hire one or two employees needs to play fair and abide by the law. It could be that offices with fewer employees do not need to follow the letter of the law under certain employment statutes. Lawyers, however, need to keep the spirit of the law in mind.

Be Smart

A golden rule to follow is never, ever hire an ex-client as an employee. The potential for conflict is there, and it's just a bad idea. If the client relationship ends smoothly, let the client go on her merry way. Everybody stays happy. If, on the other hand, a happy client turns into an unhappy employee, this might impact the lawyer-client relationship. Remember, an ex-client has several years to file a grievance.

> **Beware!**
> Before hiring anyone, take the time to read state and federal employment laws, even if your office is too small for some of them to apply.

Small office and solo lawyers get to know their clients very well. With certain friendly clients, the temptation exists to broaden the relationship into something more: a friendship, an employment situation, a sexual relationship. Resist these temptations at all costs.

Financing

Borrowing money is almost always a bad idea, but the lawyer fresh out of law school may not have the resources to start up without outside financing. There are the questions of rent and down payment, office furniture, file cabinets, copy machines, computers, facsimile machines, printers, paper products and stationery, large briefcase and small, soft briefcase, and the set of state law books and rules of procedure. These items are standard and necessary. In this age of computers and word processing, no one should borrow money in order to hire a secretary or receptionist.

Begin your search for cash with family. Try getting cash advances from relatives, especially spouses, parents, and grandparents. Better yet, work and save money before deciding to set up shop. You'll earn both money and a little experience.

> **Bright Idea**
> No matter how much money you need to borrow, keep the monthly payments as low as possible. In the beginning, frugality is the key.

The amount you need to borrow depends on the economy in your area as well as the price of adequate office space and other items you need. Find an attorney whose practice you admire. Ask that person how much money is needed to set up a small office. Get as much information and advice as possible.

When deciding where to borrow money to purchase standard items, the major consideration is the amount of the monthly payment, which should be as low as possible. The main monthly expenses are rent, telephone bill (including Yellow Pages advertising), and the loan payment. The liability insurance will be a big expense once every 12 months. During the first year of practice, these items may be very burdensome. Keep them all as low as possible. Don't go hog wild on the advertising. Keep any ad small and simple.

> **Smart Tip**
> Find sturdy, used furniture in the classifieds. Copiers, computers, fax machines, scanners, and other office machines should be purchased new with an eye to reliability and the cost of cartridges. Ask yourself, can I replace the cartridge in five minutes? Never buy office machines that are smarter than you are.

Buying used furniture from the classified section of the local newspaper is a good way to keep down start-up costs. Used desks, chairs, tables, and file cabinets can be as good as new, especially when they are secondhand teachers' desks like the kind I have in my office.

Computers, printers, telephones, copiers, and facsimile machines are best bought new.

They should be medium priced with warranties included. There is no need to get the best, top-of-the-line copier. A desk-top model will do, as long as it can handle a stack of 25 pages.

Talking to an experienced solo or small office practitioner about money is an essential step before setting up shop. If possible, find someone who practices your chosen areas of the law. She will let you know how much income to expect during the first year.

> **Smart Tip**
> Do not let a copier control your office. A new lawyer does not need a copier that stands on the floor. Choose a medium-priced desk-top model with a feeder that can handle a stack of up to 25 pages. Ask yourself, can I remove a paper jam? How much do the toner cartridges and ink cartridges cost? How often will I need to replace them?

How Much to Charge

The hardest decision to make about money is how much to charge for a retainer. This happens on a daily basis. People pay retainers grudgingly, and oftentimes those who need legal help very badly are the least able to pay. Consider referring some of these people to legal services. With the others, you must request the money up front. Charge enough to get you through ten hours.

When writing a retainer agreement, remember out-of-pocket costs such as filing fees and detective's fees. Whenever possible, leave the fee agreement open-ended, in case the matter becomes complicated and requires several appearances in court. Details should be spelled out in the retainer agreement. Ask questions to ensure the client understands what the retainer agreement says.

Suggest to the potential client that he borrow the money if he desires to retain you. If you have consulted with other lawyers in your area and have a suitable retainer in mind for someone with your years of experience, do not back down on this amount. Present the potential client with a written retainer agreement that outlines the retainer amount and how much you charge per hour. Once you have filed pleadings in court, signed by you as the attorney, the court may not let you back out just because the client refuses to pay.

> **Bright Idea**
> Decide on a fair hourly rate and charge enough up front for at least ten hours of work. Do not file any pleadings in court unless and until you have been paid the full retainer up front. Keep an eye on deadlines and statutes of limitation.

In some areas, family court matters, for example, it is tempting to charge what the market will bear, setting the price according to the wealth of the client. But this presents problems of fairness. Why should the rich pay more for the same service?

Retainer agreements often depend on the type of case being handled. For example, in family court matters I set my retainer at a fair level for everyone and charge by the hour after the retainer is used up. On the other hand, my retainer in employment law cases is quite a different animal. There the agreement involves a retainer plus contingency, which means that the clients pay a retainer up front (usually nonrefundable) and contract to pay me one-third of any settlement or 40 percent of any judgment should we win in court. The client also promises to pay all out-of-pocket expenses involved in the case: filing fees ($250 to file a lawsuit in federal court), the costs of serving the defendant, postage, and depositions, the biggest expense of all.

> **Smart Tip**
> In cases you know in advance that you will need to purchase depositions, try to get some money for costs from the client up front. Put this money in escrow.

Accident cases and some other cases may be done entirely on a contingency basis. Social Security disability and other types of practice are subject to fee arrangements that are set by law. Your fee may be a flat one, set by law, and you may not get paid unless you win!

Although depositions are absolutely necessary in cases where you are facing some kind of motion to dismiss or a motion for summary judgment, they can cost a lot, as much as three dollars per page. The client may have contracted to handle all out-of-pocket expenses, but the lawyer must be prepared to pay the court reporter when the bill comes in. It's best to be prepared in advance. When a client has been known to pay for costs in the past, you might allow them to pay after the bill for the deposition is received. In all other cases, try to get the deposition money up front and put it in escrow. Otherwise, it's possible to be stuck with a bill ranging anywhere from $75 to $1,000. That can be most unpleasant, especially for beginning lawyers.

> **Smart Tip**
> Take charge of the telephone book advertising salesperson. Demand discounts. Avoid being persuaded to buy anything more than a small—very small—ad. You will be paying for this every month! If the phone company offers discounts when you upgrade an ad, try the yearly roller coaster approach. Upgrade the second year. Then downgrade. Then upgrade the fourth year, if you can afford it.

Advertising

With advertising, as with anything else in a law practice, it would be easy to go overboard and spend too much. The opportunities for advertising are many and tempting. There may be two or three major telephone books circulating in your area. Church bulletins, military newsletters, state bar publications, and television stations all advertise lawyers, with varying degrees of effectiveness. Billboards are options in most states. Some offices send out elaborate Christmas greetings and gifts. The lawyer newly on her own will wonder how much to spend and which media to utilize. The basic rule of thumb is do what you have to do to bring in enough clients—and no more.

Telephone Book Ads

Some kind of advertisement in the largest phone book is a necessary expense. The smallest ad larger than a simple listing will do. Anything larger than a business card is a mistake for newly launched practitioners. Phone books charge every month for those advertisements, and that kind of expenditure can eat away at the profits from a small office. Put something in the phone book, but keep it small and classy. The public will equate small telephone book ads with lawyers who charge a reasonable retainer fee.

Negotiate with the telephone company for discounts. It may have a discount available for upgrading to a larger ad. Use an accordion approach. After three years in practice, upgrade to a slightly larger ad. Ask for a discount. The next year, downsize. The following year, upgrade again and negotiate for a discount.

> **Smart Tip**
> The state bar's lawyer referral service is a smart way to advertise, and its requirements keep you honest.

State Bar Referral Service

Another good way to advertise is through your state bar's lawyer referral service. These services often require a certain amount of experience in a given area of the law. They may require a minimal amount of liability insurance. Keeping current with a referral service can mean paying a yearly fee and/or a percentage of profit from each case referred that earns the lawyer money.

Referral services keep the phones ringing, and they are usually worth what they charge. They also keep the lawyer on his toes with regard to liability insurance. As soon as you have the experience to qualify, sign up.

> **Smart Tip**
> The only advertisements you really need are a small Yellow Pages ad and a listing in your state bar's referral service.

What to Avoid

The lawyer should avoid any type of advertising that he cannot afford. No one needs a full-page ad when starting out. Come to think

> **Bright Idea**
>
> Do maintain a web site, but have a friend or a spouse build it and take care of the domain fees and registration. Do not pay a service to manage a web site, because it usually charges too much.

of it, why would anyone *ever* need a full-page ad in the telephone book? Having a big ad does not equate with being a big lawyer. The lawyers with the big ads may be those who need to generate a client base—not those who are already successful. Really successful small practitioners may not advertise at all because they have enough clients already.

Keep in mind that the attorney who has a spot in the Yellow Pages does not need much more advertising. This is a litigious society, and many people need legal services. Those who are looking to pay less will search for the smaller ads. Most attorneys who have been around for a while have more work than they can handle. The problem then becomes not how to obtain clients but how to handle the clients they already have.

Having a web site may make a lawyer feel very hip and up to date in today's computer-driven society. It's probably a good idea, but it won't bring in many clients. It's not something worth spending a lot of money on. Those people it does attract will be mainly from outside the state.

The newly launched practitioner can get a web site cheaply, for example, by building one through AOL's 1-2-3 Publish® system or through Easy Publish®. Or find a computer friend to build your web site and register the domain name. Pay the friend to build you something nice. What the new lawyer should avoid absolutely is an expensive monthly fee for maintaining a web site, such as the plans offered through telephone services. These are a waste of money and not as creative as something a friend or friend's referral can build for you.

5

What They Don't Teach You in Law School

Astrange dichotomy divides our modern world, especially in the United States. We cherish our independence while we crave the help of others. Lawyers have these same conflicting feelings.

Sometime during the third, or the ninth, or the twelfth year of running a solo practice, lawyers realize that they are not islands. A solo practitioner always needs help, lots of help and advice. Young lawyers, especially, should look for mentors, those more experienced lawyers who personally know every clerk of the court, trade jokes with every judge, and share football statistics with every opposing counsel.

> **Smart Tip**
> Choose attorneys as mentors who lead the type of life you want to lead. If money is the most important thing in your professional life, find a wealthy older attorney and emulate him. If lifestyle issues matter more to you, find an honest, fun-loving attorney to give you advice.

Law school teaches how to read cases and do research. It's only after passing the bar that the new lawyer learns how to be a lawyer, how to behave in the courtroom, how the system works, which papers to file and when, how to treat the lawyer on the other side, how to work judges, how to behave like a lawyer, and how to dress. New lawyers learn that they need mentors to tell them when to get angry with the system and when to maintain control. Mentors let young lawyers know that everything is really alright when the whole world seems lost.

Law is more than books and procedures. Much of the practice of law depends on the personalities of others. Much of the law is scary and cutthroat. Influence may play a huge role in judges' decisions. It is not a profession to enter alone.

Attorneys shouldn't have medical doctors or librarians as mentors. Only other attorneys can relate to the pressures of the job, the scramble to earn money, and the demands of professional liability. Only attorneys can understand the breaking fear of receiving a letter marked "personal and confidential" from the state bar.

Mentors: You've Got to Have Them

Lawyers who treat their clients right make the best mentors; they'll probably treat you right, too. A good mentor must be someone whose research skills and courtroom style you admire.

Experienced attorneys are invaluable sources of information. Imitate them. Buy the same books they buy, copy their pleadings, and take their advice on what office equipment to purchase. Observe their client relationships and their accounting methods. Borrow their retainer agreements. If a true mentor advises you to "fire" a certain pesky client, do it right away. Do not imagine that you know more than the attorney who has practiced for 25 years, who knows more than you about *everything*. Do not think that the only good mentors are the ones who drive fancy cars (unless making money is a primary goal).

A number of attorneys have given me badly needed advice or faxed me copies of pleadings, but a true mentor is someone who does more than hand out exemplary paperwork. A true mentor teaches through example and through the way he or she lives his or her life. A mentor is someone you emulate because of his dignity or lack thereof. A mentor lives her life according to a philosophy that makes sense to you. A mentor is usually someone older who enjoys the kind of success you wish you could share.

> **Bright Idea**
> True mentors have an attitude about work and a way of dealing with clients that you admire. You can learn a lot from mentors by listening to them talk to their clients.

During the ten years I've been practicing law, I've had three true mentors: the man who was my boss for one year, my attorney landlady, and a solo attorney, a friend.

During the ten months he was my boss, my first mentor taught me a number of things about employment law, a terribly difficult subject in South Carolina. He taught me that the small law firm can beat the big law firm. He taught me to be honest with my clients' money, not to charge too much or take advantage in a settlement situation. He taught me to have friendly relations with my clients, as often as possible. Laughing and joking around with a client can be a good thing, and clients who don't like that style should look elsewhere. He taught me how to behave in the courtroom—when humor is appropriate and when to stand up and say, "Yes, sir." He taught me to treat support staff with respect. When I walked away from that job, I knew my understanding of the law had reached a higher level.

His attitude about work and about the law inspired my admiration. For clients and outsiders such as judges and opposing attorneys, he always had a smile on his face and a corny country joke. To the outside world, he didn't take life too seriously. We were having fun as we took people to court and deposing witnesses.

Inside the office he yelled too much, and I left. But I could only practice employment law on my own because I had learned so much from him.

My second mentor appeared when I rented the second floor of her building for office space. I rented two rooms, then three. She didn't charge too much rent, but she gave me a lot of advice. It was her attitude that caught my attention right away. She was always smiling and often exercising. To this day, at the age of 85, she walks 20 blocks every morning before work. And she is a good lawyer who always remembers the law correctly.

"Don't ever hate anyone," was her best piece of advice. She also advised against ever working for anyone else (if an attorney can help it). Her idea of success was congruent with mine, and she ends her work week every Friday at noon. From her I learned to avoid certain areas of practice that involve influence and dishonesty.

My third mentor gave me confidence. He had practiced law for about 20 years more than I and was running a solo law practice nearly the way I wanted to run mine. The clients felt comfortable in his office. The atmosphere was walk-in. He had a playroom strewn with kiddie videos so clients could bring their children. Although my office was (and is) a lot neater than his, I liked the idea that he made his clients feel at home.

> **Smart Tip**
> When facing a scary situation in court, look to mentors for advice or a mantra that will help you deal with the situation. True mentors give you advice that calms you down and allows you to focus on the work.

He gave the law a relaxed feeling, but he based all his arguments on solid legal research. "Look at the rule!" he bellowed whenever a legal problem surfaced and I ran to him for help. He was a true mentor because he gave me confidence, confidence to deal with difficult cases and difficult judges.

I remember sitting in his office shaking with fear. The mountain of paperwork due in court before a federal trial was completed, and I was about to plan my strategy. After listening to me describe the case, he had only one piece of advice: "Steal their fire." Explain away the weak points of your case. Make them sound like nothing. I began repeating to myself, "Steal their fire. Steal their fire!" And I repeated this phrase during the next two days of preparation and during the drive to the court. It was both a mantra and a road map that guided my every action through the trial.

I won, and my client walked away happy. Of course, my own actions led to this victory, but my mentor gave me direction and a huge dose of confidence. Besides "steal their fire," he had given me another piece of advice that still rings in my ears to this day, "You can do it!"

All three mentors enjoyed talking to their clients and treated them fairly. They went far in dispelling any myths about the lawyer as snake. Don't enter the courtroom without the guidance of mentors.

Managing a Case

Managing a case involves three basic skills: setting up and enforcing the agreement between attorney and client, organizing the file, and keeping the case moving forward in a timely manner. In happy circumstances, the case will also involve the fine art of settlement. Almost none of skills necessary to manage a case are taught in law school.

Retainer Agreement

No attorney-client relationship exists until a client signs a retainer agreement. The new attorney should look at sample retainers and think long and hard about the elements that need to be included. Some of the basic ones are:

- a description of the work to be performed, with parameters;
- the amount of the retainer agreement, which in many states cannot be nonrefundable;
- the hourly rate to be charged by the attorney after the retainer amount is exhausted;
- a contingency percentage to be collected by the attorney in case of settlement and the contingency amount owed the attorney if it goes to trial, which may not always apply;
- the circumstances under which the attorney may withdraw from the case;
- a list and/or description of costs that the attorney may charge the client, such as deposition fees, filing fees, and detective's fees;
- whether or not the attorney could associate another attorney on the case and how that associate would be paid.

> **Smart Tip**
> Through the wording of the retainer agreement, always give yourself a way to escape from a case if a client is recalcitrant about settling, refuses to communicate with the attorney, or refuses to take the advice of the attorney. Clients who behave disrespectfully in court need to be dumped.

The client should have a copy of this contract, as soon as she signs it. (The client should also be copied with all other pleadings and important correspondence.) I like to staple the original retainer agreement (signed in blue) to the back of the main manila folder in the accordion file.

Creating a File

Each case file should be recorded in at least three ways:

1. A paper (hard) copy stored in a file cabinet
2. A computer copy on the hard drive of a computer
3. A copy of the computer file on disc, zip drive, CD, or removable hard drive.

Anything less than this invites disaster.

> **Smart Tip**
> Copy the client with the retainer agreements, all pleadings, and all important correspondence. When the opposing attorney telephones you, let your client know the gist of the conversation.

> **The Whole Truth**
>
> Old files need to be stored a certain number of years before being discarded. Check with your state bar to find out how many years. Before closing a file and storing it, always inform the client, in writing, that the attorney-client relationship has ended.

An average file consists of one or more accordion folders filled with thinner manila folders. Everything is labeled with the name of the client. For example, an active file might include: Smith, Donald; Smith, Donald—pleadings; Smith, Donald—correspondence; and Smith, Donald—incident reports.

Once the file has been stored, it will also have a number and date the file was closed, which correspond to an index card, filed alphabetically by name. Stored files need to be kept at least the number of years dictated by your state bar. When an attorney gets ready to close up shop, it's easier to go back and purge all files that are more than six years old if the files are stored according to the age of the file. In order to locate a file, it's necessary to have the corresponding index cards, arranged alphabetically.

Files must be kept a certain number of years to enable attorneys to respond to grievances. When building and storing files, keep the idea of a grievance in mind: "This letter needs to be stored in hard copy and on the computer in order to prove that I wrote to the judge on this particular date and copied the opposing attorney." "The retainer agreement must be kept in one particular place to remind me of the precise understanding between me and the client." Hopefully a grievance will never occur, but preparing for one keeps the small practitioner on his toes. It's like a silent managing partner.

For billing purposes and for grievance purposes, keep a list of all hours worked, along with a description of how the time was spent. An entry might look like this:

> November 16, 2004
> Met with client and her mother
> Discussed content of the complaint
> 1 hour

Always keep in mind that the file belongs to the client. Attorneys are obliged to keep a copy of the file on record for a certain number of years, but the primary owner of the file is the client, whether she owes attorney's fees or not. When a client asks me for a copy of her file, I try to set a date that will allow me to copy everything I need for myself. If the client were to demand the file immediately, however, I

> **The Whole Truth**
>
> The client owns his file, even if he owes you money. Always be prepared to copy a file and hand it over to a client on demand, within a reasonable amount of time. When a client demands his file immediately, it always helps to explain that the bar expects attorneys to keep each file for a certain number of years. You need a few days to make a copy.

would have to turn over the hard copy right then. This is one reason why it's necessary to preserve everything possible on disk and on the hard drive of the computer.

Keeping a Case Alive

Another situation that may surprise the new lawyer is that civil cases that have been filed and served are not holy objects. They entitle the parties to nothing, no notice, no deference, no help. The lawyer is the impetus that propels the case forward. (That and the client calling the lawyer 50 times a day.)

Once a case has been filed, it is the lawyer's duty to keep it alive. The complaint must be served, properly, by the lawyer who filed it. If the defending party defaults by failing to answer the complaint, the plaintiff's attorney must notify the court by filing a notice of default. The court will not magically notice that a complaint that was served 30 days ago has not been answered. The court is busy; the court does not care. The lawyer must grab the court by the throat.

If the case is a civil matter bound for trial, the attorney must keep abreast of the roster and attend roster meetings. Clerks of court and deputy clerks of court know where to find the roster, which the attorney needs to check on a weekly basis. The roster can be online or posted at the courthouse.

The court acts like royalty. It will not take notice of *anything* that happens with a case unless one of the lawyers brings it to the court's attention. The lawyer must file notices and motions, and compose orders. One would think that in a divorce action, for example, the judge would write the final order. It is the judge, after all, who has made all the decisions. But no, the judge assigns one of the lawyers to write the final order, and it is up to the two lawyers involved to remember what happened during the trial, unless someone wishes to pay three dollars per page to order a transcript from the court reporter.

Clients tend to grow weary of cases unless something happens fast. The court system is so overcrowded, unfortunately, that keeping things moving at a snappy pace is almost impossible. There are things that can be done to keep the action going between hearings, however. The major activity is discovery: depositions, interrogatories, and requests to produce documents. Other forms of aggressive action are subpoenas, motions to throw the case out of court (by defendants), and requests for temporary relief.

When your client is the plaintiff who brings the action (also known as the aggressor), these

> **The Whole Truth**
> It's the responsibility of the plaintiff's attorney to keep a file alive by actively seeking discovery, filing motions, trying to settle the case, keeping in touch with the client, and generally attempting to resolve the matter as quickly as possible.

tactics are good strategy as long as the client is willing to pay. When the client needs to save money, however, or when the issues are divorce and child custody, too much aggressive action can harm the children and increase the hostility between the parties. Attorneys should use discovery with caution in divorce cases.

A simpler way to keep a case alive is by communicating often with the client. Be sure to answer phone messages whenever possible. Some clients seem to disappear into the woodwork. A phone call every month or two can remind the client that litigation is pending. This also keeps the attorney informed as to the client's whereabouts and what's happening in his life.

Client Control and Settlement

Settlement is almost always the best answer. This is one maxim that needs to be experienced in order to be believed. A lawyer may feel gung-ho about her chances of winning on the law and on the merits, that her client is absolutely right and there is case law supporting her position. The path to victory may seem crystal clear until the parties walk into the courtroom. Fireworks ensue. The case gets thrown out because of a technicality. Your client has a criminal record he forgot to mention. A witness fails to show up. The opposing attorney is the judge's childhood friend. Anything can happen.

The law has so many facets beyond the bare facts of the case that a judge can usually find reasons to rule either way. Case law often depends on the vagaries of the judge, which lawyer he favors or whether one lawyer comes from a large firm and the judge is worried about reappointment. Ease in making a quick decision is one factor that influences many cases. When one side's argument is clearer and easier to figure out in five minutes, the judge will often choose that argument.

Always remember that the judge is king of the courtroom. Any arbitrary decision by a judge can be overturned on appeal. However, appeals take time and money, and their outcome is very uncertain.

For these reasons, most of the time clients must be encouraged to settle if the opportunity presents itself. A settlement cannot be appealed. A settlement means money in the pocket. A settlement allows parties to move on with their lives. Particularly in divorce actions, settlement is nearly always the best option because it signals the parties' ability to compromise on such issues as caring for the children.

Unfortunately, because of television and thirst for revenge, some clients think of settlement as a sign of weakness. They've been hurt,

> **Tip...**
> **Smart Tip**
> Before agreeing to represent a client, make sure he understands that settlement is almost always the best option. Explain the reasoning behind this: settlements cannot be appealed; they equal money in the bank; they hold down legal fees and court costs.

and they don't want to give up the fight. Motions, discovery, and hearings become weapons for punishing the other party. When a settlement offer is good, the attorney's job is to convince her client that settlement equals victory. This victory is much more final and meaningful than telling her story in court or making the estranged spouse "pay" for his actions.

This does not mean that parties should accept an unjust situation or agree to pay for something they cannot afford, such as college tuition. Irrevocable agreements to pay money for a certain number of years are never acceptable. People can lose their jobs. The economy can go sour.

Under certain circumstances clients must be incited to fight, even if they are weary of the situation and long to escape from it. The attorney must make this decision. Clients who are emotionally battered and fearful of the trial process need the support of their attorneys at times like this. Nobody likes to discuss his private life in open court, but the judges have heard the same story a million times. Unless a settlement is reasonable, encourage your client to put up a strong front. Go to trial, if necessary, rather than living with regret and poverty for the rest of his life.

For the most part, however, agreements in which both parties give up something and both parties gain something symbolize the triumph of the legal system. Client control, for the most part, means encouraging a client to settle when the time is right. Mediation can be the answer. In many jurisdictions, it has even become mandatory for certain cases.

6

Settling Outside of Court

Settlement is central to the practice of law in the United States. Every day lawyers must deal with disputes and with the question of how these disputes can be resolved. These disputes almost always involve money. They can also involve child custody, plea bargaining in criminal cases, or a set of dining room furniture. Settlement can mean fixing an amount of child support, setting hours of visitation, and dividing equity in the marital home. In all of these situations, lawyers must relate to clients who have various personal problems and points of view and who may want revenge—not a negotiated settlement.

The Benefits of Settlement

While clients often resist it, settlement is a process that empowers the parties rather than the courts. The parties make the decision, rather than the judge (who has limited time available to her to consider the situation). It gives all the power to the people. Settlement should not imply weakness, as most litigants think in the beginning. It allows the client to take charge, with the backing of the court, because the settlement agreement becomes a court order.

Negotiating a settlement in an impassioned case is the most difficult thing that small practitioners can do because there are usually at least four obstacles involved: two clients and two lawyers. On any one issue, the lawyers may agree wholeheartedly, but one or more clients may nix the resolution, bringing the case back to square one.

Good lawyers are definitely more amenable to easy settlements than are the parties involved. Lawyers want to resolve disputes and get on with life. Lawyers want peace, quiet, and to collect their fees. Lawyers, at heart, want people to get along. Settlement is the very best vehicle to resolve a dispute—for the client. This is because settlement provides closure, both legally and psychologically. Settlements cannot be appealed to a higher court. Settlements mean each party is a little bit happy and a little bit dissatisfied. Settlements mean "it's over."

Smart Tip
Settlement is almost always the best option in a case when the opposing side makes a fair offer. Settlement takes power away from the judge and hands it to both parties. The best settlements occur when each side gives up something.

In the best cases, settlements can work smoothly and quickly. For example, recently I dealt with an in-house attorney at a large company. He was firm in everything he said, but he never acted like a hired gun. My client's demands were reasonable; I saw to that.

When we first spoke, I was apprehensive. We were threatening to sue his company, after all. He was on the road, eating lunch when we connected. We discussed the case in civil terms. I never spoke in a harsh voice, and neither did he. After about five conversations, we settled the matter, and both sides were happy. Had we not been able to communicate well, the lawsuit would have proceeded to court. Instead of costing his company one year's salary for one person and a few phone calls, the case might have cost them twice as much in legal fees, whether they won or lost. My "opponent" was an intelligent lawyer with a lot of savvy.

Lawyers cannot always prevail this neatly. The power to make final decisions about cases belongs, sometimes unfortunately, to the parties involved—especially the plaintiffs who bring the lawsuits in the first place. The solution to this problem, for the lawyer, is "client control," and it is a difficult, and occasionally impossible, concept to master on every occasion. Some clients simply cannot be controlled. The best lawyers gain control because they know the law and their clients do not know the law. They communicate confidence. The confident lawyer teaches the client that everything the client has heard on the outside—about litigation, about divorce, about social services—is wrong. Forget the internet and the next door neighbor's horrific experience in a divorce. Forget television! The lawyer knows more because the lawyer has been in court. He knows what he can and cannot accomplish, and he charges accordingly. His fees are realistic. He does not milk the client. His clients trust him.

Sometimes the best way to control a client is through money and threats of fees. The experienced family lawyer will say, "You can settle this child custody matter between yourselves, or you can pay a guardian $4,000 to settle it for you." There are not many clients who will choose to pay the money when it comes down to this. If the lawyer has earned the trust of the client, this tactic often convinces clients to act reasonably. The client will lay aside emotion and make difficult choices rather than pay the money and fight it out.

Still, some clients cannot be controlled. They will go on forever, like the Energizer Bunny, fueled by revenge. In the end, the client must live with a compromise (family law) or with his case being thrown out entirely by a conservative judge (employment law). Being difficult doesn't often lead to the result desired.

> **The Whole Truth**
> In order to settle a case, the attorney must have the trust of his client and reasonable control over the client. A lawyer who loses control of his client should be able to back out of the case. Any retainer agreement should give the attorney the right to drop a case if the client becomes unreasonable and refuses to accept a fair offer of settlement.

The Negotiated Settlement

In an effort to reduce case loads in the court system, speed up justice, and lower legal costs, state courts have begun requiring mediation or arbitration before a case is tried.

In South Carolina, for example, certain counties require that those who sue for $25,000 or less in damages in state court must arbitrate their case in front of a paid arbitrator who must come up with a decision. If the clients do not like the decision, they can appeal it to circuit court. Those who sue for $25,000 or more in damages and those battling over the custody of a child must go through mediation.

A new practitioner would be well advised to obtain some training in mediation or arbitration, since many of his cases will involve this type of negotiation. The best, most talented lawyers are those who manage to settle a case before it goes to trial.

Mediation

Mediation is basically an orchestrated meeting to coerce the parties into settlement. The mediator, who directs the meeting, has no actual power to force the parties to do anything. The mediator can express an opinion, put the parties in separate rooms, and convey messages back and forth, but the mediator cannot issue a binding decision. Usually this service costs $100 or more per hour. I've been in mediations where the mediator (a former judge) charged $300 per hour.

> **Smart Tip**
> The best mediators are also practitioners and experts in the area of the law of the case being mediated. To settle an auto accident case, choose a mediator who also litigates auto accidents.

When both parties are recalcitrant, mediation is a waste of time. Both parties must be willing to give up something. The best way to prepare a client for mediation is to make a list ahead of time of exactly what the client must have and where she would be willing to compromise. Be smart enough to stop the mediation, which costs your client hourly, if the situation is going nowhere.

Mediation works best when the mediator is an expert in the area of law involved in the case. So a family law litigator who acts as a mediator is the best person to help settle a family law case. When the mediator can offer an unbiased opinion on the merits of the case, his services are useful. If the mediator is solely intent on settling, with no real regard for the merits of the case, his intervention is less meaningful.

> **Smart Tip**
> Avoid the heartbreak of mediation by having both parties sign a settlement agreement if the case settles. This way, they can't go home, sleep on it, and change their minds.

One of the golden rules of mediation is that the parties should be required to sign a written agreement on the spot whenever a settlement occurs. Write the attorney's fees into the agreement. The heartbreak of mediation occurs when one of the parties goes home after an agreement takes place, sleeps on it, and then decides the next morning that she agreed to settle for too little money. She then calls her attorney. Is the agreement binding? In South Carolina it is, unless either party was coerced. When she has a written settlement agreement in hand, the attorney can enjoy her day despite that phone call, knowing the case is securely settled.

Arbitration

In arbitration, the case is actually tried before a paid arbitrator, with opening statements, closing statements, and testimony from witnesses. If the clients do not like the decision, they can appeal it to state circuit court. Arbitration may sometimes make more sense than mediation because the arbitrator issues a decision. Even if they decide to appeal the results, clients can see how their case will play out in front of an audience and whether they have enough evidence to win over a jury. And the arbitrator's decision becomes part of the court file. Although the jury does not have access to this decision, the judge—and the judge's clerk—see it

> **The Whole Truth**
> Arbitration (nonbinding) is somewhat less useful than mediation because the decision of the arbitrator can be appealed. The process is like a trial before the trial.

(Court-ordered arbitration should not be confused with binding arbitration, which is often part of a contractual agreement. Binding arbitration cannot be appealed. It is a final decision.)

The problem with arbitration is precisely that it can be appealed. Although there is an official decision, there is no meeting of the minds between the parties. Mediation (when it works correctly) involves a settlement and finality, an end to the case, whereas arbitration is just the first decision in a string of decisions that can be appealed to a higher authority. The appeal process may mean that the prevailing party must wait months, even years, to see any money. Arbitration adds one more rung to the opportunity to be heard—and possibly denied. If you do win, there's always the chance the other side will appeal. In the end, arbitration is not much better than trying the case.

7

Playing Well with Others

Much of the practice of law depends on dealing with other professionals such as doctors, pharmacists, police officers, accountants, and social workers and persuading them to furnish information. You may want paperwork from them, or you may want them to appear in court as witnesses. Sometimes you just want something explained. As a lawyer, you have to know a few things besides the law. Maybe it's engineering, medicine, or how to compute the present value of future wages. Lawyers with dual degrees are lucky. The rest have to rely on research or (better yet) the advice of another professional.

Relationships with Other Professionals

> **Bright Idea**
> Consider the practicality of getting a dual degree in another field, such as business, social work, or human resource management, if your university offers such opportunities to law students. These degrees double your chances of finding a job, and the extra knowledge will make you a better lawyer.

Relationships with professionals in other fields is also critical to a lawyer's success. Treating others decently and respectfully is likely to result in your being treated decently and respectfully—and being able to get some expert help when you need it. And having friends is never a bad idea.

Doctors

Once you begin practicing law, you will be amazed at how often you wish you had a medical degree. Medical records play a huge role in many legal cases: slip-and-fall litigation, Social Security disability claims, car accidents, medical malpractice, divorce, child custody, criminal defense, and any sort of litigation that claims medical damages. With the new HIPAA (Health Insurance Portability and Accountability Act) laws regarding the confidentiality of patient information, medical records and counselors' notes have become increasingly difficult to obtain. But for the small practitioner, they are necessary, and often expensive. You have to get them, and you have to know how to read them.

> **Smart Tip**
> Collect several medical release forms from hospitals in your area. Using these as examples, compose a general medical release of your own that meets all the HIPAA requirements.

Begin collecting the proper release forms from medical facilities in your area. Compose a general medical release that meets all the HIPAA requirements, indicating what the records are for, who is to receive them, for how long the release is good, and exactly what portion of the records is needed.

Some medical records are handwritten and nearly impossible to read. At other offices, doctors have begun using medical record systems that allow them to type in everything and print it out in a highly legible form. The Veterans Hospital in my area is a fine example. They went from dot matrix notes on attached, continuous printouts to beautifully printed notes that always include a page number, a date, and the name of the patient.

Doctors blame lawyers for their outrageous medical malpractice insurance rates and for the fact that patients can hold the lawsuits over their heads. Although lawyers are also victims of the same system, doctors do not always see this. They are not always favorably inclined toward lawyers. This is unfortunate for lawyers because medical opinions and medical notes are so often crucial to the practice of law.

There are two ways to dam the dislike flowing from doctors to attorneys. The first is obvious: lawyers should make friends with as many doctors as possible. Explain to them the work that lawyers do. Stay away from the topic of malpractice lawsuits. Mention how lawyers depend on doctors for expert opinions, medical records, and determinations of disability.

The second way to stem the distrust is to have both doctors and lawyers involved in certain continuing legal education courses. Lawyers must take a certain number of continuing education hours each year in order to remain current members of the bar. Some of these courses should be designed to entice doctors to attend or include medical doctors as speakers. The obvious areas of the law that spring to mind are worker's compensation, Social Security disability, Medicare and Medicaid, and automobile accidents.

Medicare and Medicaid reporting are areas which interest both doctors and lawyers. Perhaps the local American Medical Association and the state bar could get together and form joint legal/medical continuing legal education courses. The speakers could include both doctors and lawyers. The questions from the audience would be dynamic.

Because doctors may distrust lawyers, the small practitioner needs to think outside the box in terms of medical expert testimony. A registered nurse often has knowledge of a particular medical topic that is just as good as a doctor's knowledge. And nurses may be more articulate than doctors. They may cost less, too. A nurse with material knowledge of the incident, who actually worked on the case, is a gold mine. A nurse retained as an expert, from outside the situation, might also be a viable alternative.

> **Smart Tip**
> Become friendly with doctors. Suggest that your state bar sponsor continuing legal education courses that feature doctors as speakers on such topics as Social Security disability and auto accidents.

Keep in mind, however, that medical doctors often trump other, lesser health professionals. A judge will probably give more weight to the testimony of a medical doctor or dentist than he gives to the testimony of a nurse, all other factors being equal.

Social Workers and Therapists

In today's stressful society, psychological therapists and counselors play a large role in the life of the public and the process of law. These people may be psychiatrists, psychologists, social workers, or practitioners with bachelor's degrees in clinical therapy. Clients sometimes present themselves with mental problems or find themselves developing them during the course of a lawsuit such as those involving divorce. They may need therapy, or they're already in therapy. A lawyer needs to be familiar with basic psychological terminology (such as "psychosis," "personality disorder," "traumatic stress disorder," "schizophrenia") as well as the current faddish psychotropic drugs that are on the market—legal as well as illegal. A lawyer needs to recognize when alcohol is being used as self-medication. The lawyer who has taken a few college courses in psychology is ahead of the game.

Social worker therapists, who often have an interest in public policy, can be much friendlier toward lawyers than psychiatrists, who are medical doctors. Social workers are often willing to work with lawyers. Public policy, in fact, is part of their training. Hence, they may be willing to part with their counseling records

> **Smart Tip**
> If you're still in college and plan to become a lawyer someday, take as many abnormal psychology courses as possible. You're going to need them.

more easily and more cheaply. They will talk with lawyers on the phone if they sense the lawyer has the client's best interest at heart. Social workers may even collaborate with lawyers.

When social workers are respected members of the community used to testifying in court, they can benefit the case to no end. If the allegations in your complaint include mental problems, think of calling a social worker/therapist as an expert.

The small practitioner who thinks of becoming a lobbyist for social causes should definitely become friendly with social workers. They are champions of the indigent and powerless. In the past, social workers have been more prominent in government. President Franklin Delano Roosevelt had many social workers on his staff, including Harry Hopkins and Frances Perkins. Together they initiated such crucial programs as Social Security and Medicare/Medicaid and the Works Progress Administration. Social workers often attempt to lobby the government themselves, and they can be found working in every area of public service.

Accountants

Besides medical information, the other areas of knowledge that universally benefit lawyers are accounting and taxation. Sure, lawyers have to take tax law in school, but

> **Bright Idea**
> Find a reasonable accountant to help figure your taxes. Use that same accountant on behalf of a client to figure the tax ramifications of a settlement. Make this calculation available to your client before finalizing the settlement.

its importance doesn't become clear until you have to figure the tax ramifications of a settlement. How much of that money will the client have to pay in taxes? Call a friendly accountant.

Although lawyers need to read the tax laws themselves, the surest way to check and double check the tax ramifications before signing that agreement is to call an accountant. Being friendly with one or two accountants is a great idea, almost a necessity for the small practitioner. They can keep us honest and suggest new and creative solutions.

Divorce cases involving the division of retirement assets always have tax ramifications. Nobody should agree to anything unless and until they have checked with an accountant. For example, I often instruct a client to call the accountant they use while I'm checking with my own CPA. Getting the same answer twice is a great assurance.

Law Enforcement Officials

Policemen in the United States face very difficult conditions. They often do not receive sufficient training, considering the dangerous work they perform. They also may be underpaid.

Lawyers often rely on policemen, and getting their cooperation is crucial for both the criminal defense attorney and the civil practitioner. Policemen often have to testify in court. They enforce court orders. They write the incident reports which may be the only record available that violence has occurred. The lawyer who chooses to represent policemen and their interests has a definite advantage in the court system. Consider offering your legal services to the local police fraternity. For the employment lawyer, representing policemen in trouble is a wise career move.

> **Smart Tip**
> Use the sheriff's office to serve papers when you aren't in a big hurry. It is much cheaper than private process servers, but slower and less reliable.

Whenever papers need to be served, the county sheriff's office is often the cheapest alternative. Call the civil process division. Their prices can be three times cheaper than a private process server. The problem with using the sheriff is that they are not very timely. If the papers need to be served by next month, send them to the sheriff's office. If they need to be served today, call a private process server.

Relationships with Legal Professionals

The legal profession is a hierarchy, and it behooves young lawyers, especially those in small practices without large internal support systems, to have the support of other lawyers outside their own office. Everyone knows it's important to have the respect of judges; not everyone knows immediately how important the respect, and thus cooperation, of others in the system is. And, sometimes, it is not always apparent to the small practice lawyer, who may be a loner or a contrarian, how important ties to colleagues are.

Clerks of Court

The need to relate well to other professionals applies doubly when it comes to people who work at the courthouses. These workers hold the keys to your cases, and they have direct contact with the judges (who are obviously the most important people to get along with on a professional level).

Fledgling lawyers graduate from law school expecting to find more respect at the courthouse than they will have. There may be some underlying contempt court reporters, clerks of court, and assistant clerks of court have for lawyers and all the frustrating work lawyers do. People who work in the clerk's office are still willing to help lawyers—but for a price.

Clerks of court wish lawyers to acknowledge that the clerks are in control. No problem, really. An experienced lawyer will readily admit the importance of the clerks of court because it is the plain truth and because other practicing lawyers see it so clearly. It is a fact that cannot be denied. You and I depend on them and should bow down to them. Clerks maintain the files. The case boils down to the contents of the file. If something isn't on file at the courthouse, it never happened.

The relationship between lawyers and clerks of court resembles, somewhat, the relationship between nurses and doctors. A more experienced registered nurse might have the utmost contempt for a new resident doctor or the medical student. The nurse knows the ropes. The nurse knows how to treat patients. Along comes the upstart doctor, who will eventually make much more money than the nurse but who now knows practically nothing about patient care. He is the medical student on rotation who blushes at the sight of a naked pregnant woman. The nurse just stands back and rolls her eyes.

Clerks of court and their associates are not supposed to give anyone legal advice, but they can be a font of information about scheduling

> **Smart Tip**
> At all times recognize that clerks of court control the scheduling of hearings and the filing of cases. To a large extent, they are in control.

problems, basic procedural issues, and how to set up a hearing. Clerks have daily contact with all the judges. Knowing the clerks' names and their direct telephone numbers is a very good idea. For example, when one of your clients depends on the clerk of court's office to supply him with child support, you will need to know the name and direct line of the assistant clerk in charge of child support.

Your Peers

Attorneys, and especially small practitioners, are the only people who can truly understand what you do all day, the pressures and the rewards. Psychologists and certified public accountants might come close, but lawyers are the only professionals who truly understand other lawyers. And they are also people who can help you with legal questions or referrals.

Law school graduates who choose to set up small practices are not usually people who join fraternities and sororities. They may not be joiners at all, preferring to broadcast their own opinions, and little inclined to compromise.

Once involved in a small practice, however, it becomes abundantly clear that relationships with other attorneys, whether they be blood relationships, friendships, social contacts, or ties formed on the job or through volunteering, are vitally important. If two attorneys' children know each other, that's an advantage. If the attorneys play tennis together, that's even better. Serving on a board with other legal professionals means that lawyers can grow comfortable with each others' personalities and politics—or at least know what to expect. Familiarity that forms outside of the courtroom has benefits, including more money for the small practitioner, more work, and more success. It makes life easier.

The Benefits of Networking

Ties with legal professionals outside of the courtroom are beneficial for a variety of reasons:

- The lawyer, especially the solo lawyer, has someone to talk to about her cases, a springboard for ideas. You may need to advise your client to declare bankruptcy but know nothing about the procedure. If you have an attorney-friend who is a bankruptcy expert, you can give her a call, pick her brain. Two attorney friends who are intimate enough can exchange impressions of judges, other attorneys, and the legal climate in general. Such conversations tend to be both cathartic and reassuring. If both attorneys think that Judge X is a nitwit, that says something.
- Attorney friends can refer cases to you, and you to them.
- The lawyer may find himself working on a particular case with an attorney friend. The friend might act as mediator, guardian, or opposing counsel. In

such situations, whenever two attorneys know each other from the outside, negotiations become easier. They waste less time breaking the ice. Each side knows how honest the other tends to be.

- The attorney acquaintance may become a judge someday.

Imagine a situation in which you, the lawyer, are working on a particularly testy divorce involving child custody. The parties are fighting bitterly over custody of two young children, and compromise or settlement looks unlikely. Both parents are average citizens, working at decent jobs, and neither has a drug problem or a criminal record. It is obvious to everyone that the opinion of the guardian *ad litem* will play a major role in directing the judge as to which party should get custody.

The judge consults a list of qualified guardians and chooses one who belongs to the same tennis club as you. You and the guardian have taken some clinics together and played opposite each other in a couple of tournaments. There is nothing resembling friendship between the two of you that might create a conflict of interest in this case, yet you feel confident that the newly-appointed guardian is a pleasant, fair individual.

What this situation gives you is a reassuring story to tell your client, "I know this guardian because we've played tennis a couple of times. She was gracious about conceding points, and I could tell that she had her priorities straight. She and I belong to the same tennis club."

This connection can put the client at ease. He will feel less fearful about inviting the guardian into his house because he will remember, "This guardian knows my attorney." The client feels better than if he had heard you say, "I know nothing about this guardian; I never met her. We'll just have to play it by ear."

Developing Connections

There are many ways to develop connections with other attorneys. Be involved in adult sports activities such as tennis leagues, soccer, yoga classes, basketball, bicycling, rowing, or swimming. Organized team sports are best. The more social the activity, the more fun it tends to be and the more it builds those connections. Running marathons is probably great for the body and wonderful for the psyche, but loner sports do nothing to increase an attorney's visibility or open him up to the public. Volunteering at adult sporting events tends to give an even broader profile.

If you have children, becoming a leader in their activities tends to put you in contact with lots of parents, some of whom could be other attorneys. Leading a pack of Cub Scouts connects you with a wide web of people, as well as being fun and creating a positive public image. It's also a heck of a lot of work—almost a second career. For those who lack the time to invest in such an undertaking, simply attending all of her daughter's basketball games forces her out of the office and into the wide, wide world.

> **The Whole Truth**
>
> Small practitioners, more than lawyers in large firms, must become Renaissance men and women, cultivating friendships and leisure activities that involve them in the community and put them in touch with other professionals.

Talking to the other parents and to the children encourages the attorney to be more open and available, a better person.

All work and no play make Jane or Jack a dull attorney. This applies doubly to the small practitioner who, more than his counterparts at large firms, must be a well-rounded individual in order to relate to his clients. It would be easy to take on a ton of cases and drown in work at a small office, but that is not an intelligent idea. Clients who approach small firms are looking for a human being, not an attorney robot. Clients find it easier to talk to an attorney who plays bridge on the weekends rather than someone who spent the last 72 hours writing a brief.

Volunteering for board memberships, speaking to school groups, and participating in charities such as Habitat for Humanity are other ways to meet people, make connections, and satisfy the soul. Finding one charity and sticking with it tends to be easier and more satisfying than dabbling in several. For the attorney who has little free time, yearly participation in the law school's moot court competition will provide contact with attorneys in a meaningful setting—possibly the same attorneys year after year. The other attorneys realize you're donating your time because they are doing the same. Even this minimal amount of participation leads to respect and recognition.

Another easy way to meet attorneys is to join any relevant special bar association, such as the women lawyers' group in your area or the black lawyers' association. Often the state bar has subcommittees such as the committee on small and solo practices or the tax law group. These committees provide the opportunity to interface solely with other lawyers—and to get a free lunch.

A new attorney's oath in the state of South Carolina requires that attorneys treat each other with respect. This attitude is much easier to adopt when attorneys know each other outside the heated atmosphere of litigation.

This is not to say that attorneys should use friendships to influence what happens in the courtroom or to forge settlements. Close friendships with judges—when the attorney and the judge know each other well enough to eat dinner at each other's houses, for example—might never be possible when the attorney and the judge practice in the same courtroom. Likewise, close friendships between opposing attorneys could create the situation clients fear most: deal making behind the client's back. Many a fair and just settlement has been compromised because of client fears that the attorneys are secretly plotting to end the case. Small practice lawyers need to keep in mind that their clients may have come to them not only because their fees are cheaper but also because they want to avoid the old-boy network they believe exists at larger firms. Clients purchase their attorney's loyalty as well as their advice, and they don't want either to be undermined by a relationship with the opposing party's attorney.

Acquaintances with other legal professionals are very important, nonetheless, and the small practitioner needs to cultivate them. This does not mean conforming. This does not mean becoming a suit or a robot simply to please others. This *does* mean that small-practice lawyers should involve themselves in the larger world while maintaining their integrity. Let the world know who you are and what you stand for. Make yourself known and visible. Honesty is the best form of advertising.

> **Smart Tip**
> Community involvement helps attorneys understand their clients better. It's also a good way to advertise yourself and your law practice.

8

Using the Library and the Internet

In depth research for any federal hearing, an appeal, or a trial means finding families of cases on the same subject. There are a few hard and fast rules. Whenever you use a case, you must Shepardize it first to make sure it's still good law and hasn't been overturned by any subsequent case. If you're looking at statutes using book research, you must cross-check the pocket parts for the latest version of a law that may have been updated before the book was reprinted.

Until recently law school librarians, who are usually attorneys, taught research using the books in the law school library. They did an excellent job. Legal research, done from books, is very straightforward, divided into state statutes and federal statutes, state cases and federal cases, regulations, and the easy cross-reference of all of these.

> **Smart Tip**
> Begin your research online, using a free search engine such as FindLaw. With a couple of cases in hand, head to the nearest law library to finish off the process. Be sure to Shepardize the cases.

Today, many larger law firms rely on expensive computer research engines such as Westlaw, that charge by the minute or by the month. Although there are less expensive search engines such as Loislaw, the small practice may well not be able to afford any such luxury in the beginning years of practice. This need not be a disadvantage.

Computer search engines tend to miss the point of many cases because they search by key word or phrase. The cases sometimes seem to be indexed by the wrong phrase or by one that misses the point of the case that the researcher is searching for. Searches often yield results that are too broad. Searching by a common key phrase such as "child custody" tends to bring up an enormous list of cases in any state.

Legal research is best done by using a chain of ideas: one case on point that leads to other cases on point, either because the first case refers to the second case or because Shepardizing the first case leads to the cases on point that follow. The key is finding that start-up case and then resorting to the books. Library research takes time, but it's time better spent than surfing the web or a legal search engine for relevant cases.

One way to get that seminal case is to begin with a free online search engine such as FindLaw. The biggest law school in your state might also have its library online for free browsing, which could provide an excellent start to any research. Another place to find start-up cases is the footnotes to the state statutes that you have in your office. The most obvious place is within pleadings written by opposing counsel, which must be answered. Which cases has the enemy cited?

> **Bright Idea**
> Purchase a set of state statutes (keep them updated), a set of state and federal rules, and whatever specialty books you need for your law office.

With one or two cases in hand, the small practitioner should, ideally, head to a good law library to complete the research process. Book research yields different and better results than online research. Larger law firms that rely on Westlaw often miss cases that are indexed in pocket parts at the library.

Lawyers must own legal books, but not an entire library. Most small practices need to purchase a set of state statutes and keep it updated. They also need a copy of the federal and state procedures, including civil and criminal, appellate procedure, and family law procedure. Once the lawyer has decided on major areas of practice, a book or two outlining that area of the law can be a nice addition to any library and provide starting points for research. Look for subject-matter books recommended by mentors or colleagues. Reading a well-written chapter on alimony, for example, that includes case law is the easiest way to do quick research before a hearing. Make sure the books are up-to-date. Warning: this quickie research will not suffice in federal court or in an appellate situation, where the clerks are plentiful and judges well informed.

> **Smart Tip**
> Read the state advance sheets online once a week. If you respond better to hard copy, order the advance sheets to be mailed to your office. The newspaper *Lawyers Weekly* is another good way to keep abreast of the latest case law.

Advance sheets, either federal or state, are another nice addition to any law library. Lawyers have to read them anyway, so they might as well arrive in the mail. Advance sheets provide the latest case law, and judges have been known to chastise lawyers who have missed something by not reading them religiously.

A smart practice is to keep files of clippings from advance sheets or newspaper ads regarding cases that fall into your area of interest. Employment lawyers might maintain a file labeled "Employment law: Age discrimination" that contains articles on that subject. A file on "Jury selection" will come in handy during the fury of trial preparation, when you need to lay your hands on the latest rulings on that subject.

Beyond that, it is a fabulous idea to situate your law practice near a law library, either at the closest law school or the state supreme court building. Despite all the online capabilities, book research is often the best, quickest way to back up a brief, especially if you have one or two relevant cases (either for or against your position) to start from. Legal research is a continuous process of cross-referencing.

In short, the best way to do research is by beginning online or with a recent case from an advance sheet and then finishing up the process at the library where you can feel, smell, and touch the law books. Research is also a stress reliever. Burying yourself in the library is an ideal way to escape the office telephone without experiencing any guilt.

9

Get a Life

Avoid taking on too many cases. That is an absolutely vital rule for small legal practitioners. How much work is too much is something that the lawyer must decide based on family responsibilities, outside interests, and the fact that all work and no play make Jack or Jill a terrible lawyer. No client wants to accept counsel from someone who lacks the sense to get out and breathe the fresh air once in a while. What good is advice on child rearing from a father who never sees his children?

A work overload can also be an ethical problem. Handling too many cases lands attorneys in trouble with their clients and the bar. Clients tend to file grievances when their cases are neglected. An unwieldy case load causes attorneys to miss deadlines and skimp on research. All of this leads to trouble.

> **Smart Tip**
> Avoid taking on too many cases. Work overload can become an ethical issue, and it makes attorneys less skillful at interacting with their clients.

Time Management for Work

The best way to accomplish time management is to limit telephone access to your office. Maintain no more than one line that the public can call in on. The second telephone line to the office should be for the facsimile machine and internet access only.

When you're working on a brief or preparing for a trial, do not answer the telephone. Answering the phone leads to appointments with potential clients, which leads to new cases. New cases lead to more money, but the money is not worth it when the attorney is overworked. If the bank balance matters more than your sanity, it's time to reorganize your expenses and your priorities. Stop that cleaning service. Terminate the file clerk. Look for cheaper office space.

The small practitioner should only take on big, time-consuming cases when the payoff is sure to be good. Exercise stringent screening methods when considering these cases. An office that relies on a regular income must have a balance between quick, easy cases and those taken on because they might result in quite a bit of money in a couple of years. A sensible balance might be 25 quick and easy cases to every one big and interesting case. Keep in mind that the big, interesting cases tend to divert your attention from the quick, easy cases that bring in regular money. Too much diversion can threaten the existence of your practice.

> **Smart Tip**
> Limit the big cases by exercising stringent screening of clients at the telephone level. Don't invite anyone into your office who doesn't have a terrific lawsuit or who cannot pay the retainer.

Sometimes, at the end of the day, it's better to pack up a file and take it home to work on later. Have a computer setup at home that allows you to carry cases from the office to home on a CD or jump drive and work on them after dinner. Taking a break to eat with family clears your mind and takes off some of the pressure. This schedule also applies to weekends. Set time limits to make the homework less daunting. "I shall work on this case between 2 P.M. and 4 P.M. on Sunday, but no longer."

A portable desk calendar is the secret to efficient time management. Some people use electronic organizers, but they may crash and burn. Anything as ephemeral as an electronic organizer or a computer calendar should be backed up by a paper calendar that fits into a briefcase. The use of two calendars tends to decrease the cost of liability insurance. Insurance companies want attorneys to have a back-up so that they don't forget deadlines and court dates.

Be sure that the desk calendar includes plenty of tennis dates, yoga classes, and lunches out with friends. The appearance of the desk calendar is an accurate measure of the attorney's sanity. When it begins to look crazy with appointments and commitments, the attorney will look crazy, too.

Balancing the Books

One of the most difficult tasks for the small practitioner is making time for balancing the books. Attorneys who use Quicken or other money management programs have to set aside time each week or each month to enter income and expenditures into the program. This usually requires at least an hour of time. One way to insure that this schedule gets followed is to have Quicken on the home computer and save that task for a Sunday afternoon at the end of each month. As unappetizing as this sounds, it's important to stay up-to-date in order to itemize the amount of money that has been paid by each client, and the expenses associated with each case. Tag each entry with the name of the case. Keeping up with this task tends to save time and headaches at tax time.

> **Smart Tip**
> Set aside time for organizing finances, and pay all the bills yourself. Do not delegate financial responsibilities to a secretary or paralegal. That opens the door to embezzlement.

Scheduling Non-Work Activities

Solo practitioners or small office partners have the luxury of taking time off for family, pleasure, or sanity. That's always been one of the chief benefits of a small practice and one of its chief attractions.

You can make time for children's school activities or be home with the kids when they have days off from school. The key to making time for the kids is early planning. When the school calendars come out, sit down with the office desk calendar and mark every day when Sally has a vacation or a teacher in-service day. This way the off days won't sneak up on you. With a calendar marked like this, you can attempt to avoid scheduling court appearances when Sally is home from school.

If you need it, use the calendar planning method to schedule a personal time/sanity day off each month. Without a secretary in the office, nobody has to know about this personal day except you and your family. Feeling overwhelmed? Take a day off to stare at dust bunnies or attend a vacuous movie. It's a much better (and cheaper) solution.

> **Smart Tip**
>
> Schedule yourself a personal day off every month to go to the movies, read, exercise, play tennis, or do nothing. It will save your sanity.

Smart time management involves the management of more than work activities. Every well-balanced life has several components: family, work, friends, exercise, and creative activities such as writing, painting, or building furniture. Many people include spiritual activities in this mix, such as attending church or synagogue. Some attorneys are part of the dating scene. Others must fit in time for a favorite charity. The important thing is to build a life you love to live.

10

Representing Clients

If practicing law is an art form, then the clients are the artist's medium, the clay, the paint, the found artifact. The most fascinating part of practicing law is meeting the colorful people who hire you and who trust you to guide them through their problems. The attorney who likes his clients, who shares humor with them, and finds them interesting will be fulfilled in his job. One of the great satisfactions of lawyering is experiencing the gratitude of a client. The thank-you notes and Christmas cards are gratifying.

Lawyers become involved in every aspect of their clients' lives: the financial, medical, relationship, and creative sides. All of these sides factor into a client's legal problems. The good lawyer gathers as much information as possible and offers solutions from every angle. The biggest question in the legal world is, "How do I solve this problem?" The answer does not always lie in litigating the case, because oftentimes a trial can make the client's life miserable.

Client Control

A major task of being a lawyer is giving clients advice. Good clients are the ones who take direction. Bad clients think of you as a hired gun and want to run the show themselves. Only a client can decide to settle, but the lawyer needs to be the architect of the case and make decisions as to how to proceed. It's not always possible for the lawyer to divorce himself from bad clients. What the lawyer *can* do is to write something into the retainer agreement that gives the attorney the power to withdraw from the case if the relationship with the client deteriorates or if the chances of winning appear to be too slight to make the case worth continuing. Discuss this portion of the retainer agreement with every client. Make sure she understands that the attorney expects cooperation and that the client will follow direction.

> **Smart Tip**
> Write your retainer agreements so that you can opt out of a case if the client refuses to accept a fair offer of settlement. The client who wants to try the case purely for revenge is out of control and undesirable.

Client Who Thinks He's a Lawyer

In this age of the internet and quick computer research, many clients enter the lawyer's office convinced they know something about the law. The statutes are written in plain English, after all, and they are available through FindLaw and other such internet services. Armed with these statutes and advice from his neighbor (who got divorced last year and now knows *everything* about *every* divorce), the client is convinced he could handle the entire case himself. He just needs somebody to file the paperwork in court.

This client, of course, is misinformed. The client has never read any case law; doesn't know what it is. He may never have set foot in a courtroom and knows nothing about legal procedure. (Serve the papers? What does that mean?) Yet he's convinced he could win. The lawyer will be amazed at how many people operate under this delusion.

The lawyer's first job is to convince the client to stop listening to those who are uninformed about the law. The lawyer's second, more difficult task is to convince the client to listen to him. This problem will continue throughout the case unless the lawyer puts his foot down. "I run the case, Mr. Client. It's my way or the highway." The client must take advice; the client must take orders from the attorney.

> **The Whole Truth**
> In this day of the internet and television lawyering, many clients are convinced they know more than their attorney. The client does know more about the facts of the case, but not about the complexities of the law.

With that said, a key element of caring for clients is listening to them. The clients are the ones most familiar with the facts. Ask them what happened and ask them often. Show genuine interest in what the clients have to say, especially when they are admitting wrongdoing. The attorney who walks into family court uninformed about his client's adultery is in trouble. Listen to your clients. Consider their opinions and give them the proper weight. An attorney with only half a picture of what's going on in a case walks into court at a disadvantage.

Vengeful Client

Any attorney–client relationship can turn sour. No matter how friendly the client may seem, the attorney must remember at all times that this client could sue her for making an error. This is why old client files must be stored for many years. This is why the attorney must document everything she does and communicate in writing with the client whenever possible.

There are several rules the lawyer must follow in order to cover herself. First, keep an up-to-date computer list of hours worked on the case. This list should include telephone calls, meetings with the client, pleadings filed, anything. Besides being an instrument for billing, it allows the attorney to reconstruct the progression of the case. This list of hours is useful every time a client telephones and asks, "What's going on with my case?"

Second, make sure the client stays informed of what is happening on the case. If the opposing lawyer calls and says something interesting, inform your client of the gist of the conversation. This can be done by letter or by telephone call. Some clients are suspicious that their lawyer will make a deal with the opposing attorney, thus cheating the client out of money and ruining the client's life. Allay the client's suspicions by keeping him informed at all times, and by being honest.

Protecting Yourself

In order to protect yourself:
- Keep an accurate list of all hours worked on each case.
- Inform the client of everything that happens on the case; copy her with pleadings and correspondence; be honest about mistakes.
- Make sure that your paper files and your computer files are complete and up to date.
- Keep a copy of every file for six years, or however many years your state bar requires.
- Mark all deadlines on your calendar.

Keeping accurate computer files and paper files that include all pleadings and correspondence can't be emphasized enough. This will be necessary during the case and may come in handy later after the case is over if the client brings a grievance. The case file belongs to the client, but *never* turn the case file over to the client without making a copy.

Make sure your calendars are up to date. Whenever a deadline occurs, mark it on your calendar. Record meetings with clients, along with telephone numbers, and cross out the meeting if the client is a no show.

If something goes haywire in the case, inform the client immediately, even if it means incriminating yourself. Everyone makes mistakes. Clients can be forgiving or unforgiving, but they all hate being deceived.

If this is your first time working on a particular type of case, make sure the client is aware of that fact before he signs a retainer agreement. Give the client a chance to find another more experienced attorney. There's always a first time for everything, but make sure you have a mentor or a consulting attorney nearby to guide you through the procedure.

Compound Client

The compound client never comes to the attorney's office alone. She arrives with a partner, a parent, or a coterie—a group of friends or relatives who act as a unit, sitting, standing, and listening in perfect syncopation. Like a hive of bees, this aggregate client does nothing alone. Each member speaks for the group, and each member listens for the group. They pool their resources before making a decision. They think together.

The problem with the compound client is deciding whom to address. Talking to the client alone does not work. The client is never alone, for one thing. For another, the decision whether to hire and trust the attorney will be made by the group. The lawyer must swivel his head and bifurcate his line of vision to address everyone at once. Make sure to get the names of everyone in the room. Talk to each person in the room. They are all interconnected.

The decision to hire or fire the attorney will not be made until the group gets a chance to be alone and talk among themselves. Do not be surprised at latent hostility that becomes apparent only after the group has left the room. A silent member of the group may be seething at every word the lawyer says. The compound client believes that there is strength in numbers, and they take this concept to heart.

Mother–Daughter Compound Client

A young woman seeking a divorce or child custody may arrive at the initial meeting with her mother. If the mother does all the talking, the lawyer should be extremely careful. Probably the mother has agreed to pay the attorney's fees. The mother will be making all the decisions. She will decide which attorney to select and what terms the daughter seeks in the lawsuit. If the mother herself is divorced, she may be the factor that precipitated the divorce or separation in the first place.

In these situations, the lawyer can do nothing but try and please the mother. This is essential, unless the daughter independently decides to separate herself from the mother. The mother makes believe that the daughter has a say in some matters, but this is often a pretense. The number of times that the daughter visits the attorney on her own shows the level of the daughter's independence.

> **The Whole Truth**
> Compound clients are dangerous because they are twice as difficult to please and twice as easy to anger.

Client with Money Problems

To the outsider, it may seem at first that the client with low income would have more money problems than any other—in other words, more debt. In general, however, the client with low income faces the problem of obtaining essential goods and services—which is a different problem. The problem faced by the low-income client is lack of money—not debt or poor money management. The client with low income usually realizes what he or she cannot afford and resists buying it. Plus, she cannot get any credit.

Some middle-class clients, on the other hand, do not show such restraint. They see what they cannot afford, and they buy it anyway, digging themselves into a hole. The

> **The Whole Truth**
> Many middle-class Americans who are living high on the hog are actually overburdened with debt. Litigation, especially divorce, puts an added strain on their finances.

higher the income, the worse may be the temptation. The newer the money, the higher the fever to spend it. People whose grandparents were rich, or at least middle class, are less likely to fall into the debt trap.

Overspending has become a national sickness in the United States. But overspending is more a matter of personality than anything else. People who are born cheap—for whatever reason (maybe it's genetic)—never fall into the debt trap unless faced with catastrophe. People who are born to spend, on the other hand, can dig themselves into a hole by merely looking at an American Express card. They don't see the purchase of a new Land Rover as an extravagance. To them, it's a necessity—the same as buying a loaf of bread. If the neighbor has a Land Rover, the spender reasons, I must have a Land Rover.

The tendency to overspend comes into the forefront during divorce. Divorce is both an economic and emotional parting of the ways, and judges in South Carolina, for example, look very closely at the financial declaration that each party must file with the court before the first hearing. This declaration lays out a party's monthly income, expenses, and indebtedness. If the parties have a high amount of debt, the court will look seriously at this and order the parties to do something about it. Debts, like assets, are marital property to be divided between the divorcing parties.

The lawyer should talk to the client about spending less and staying out of debt. Discourage the use of credit cards. Talk enthusiastically about paying for things up front, with cash. Get on your soap box about it.

Sick Client

All attorneys must be prepared to deal with clients who are weakened by addiction, illness, or mental incapacity. These clients need representation in the legal system more than well individuals. In addition, they need an attorneys who can step out of the box and give them help in areas other than the courtroom arena.

Addicted Client

One of the horrors of modern society is the number of people addicted to alcohol or drugs. "Drugs" are not merely illicit products like heroin or marijuana. Doctors' prescription of Prozac, Zoloft, and the like has made prescription drugs nearly as much a problem as illegal drugs. The small practitioner will notice that many clients walk into the office acting like zombies, their reaction times slowed. They complain of memory lapses and sexual dysfunction. Their eyes are glazed over. They act dull rather than alert. They seem distracted and slightly out of touch with reality.

> **The Whole Truth**
> Practicing law in a small practice makes you wish you had both a medical degree and a PhD in psychology.

The drugged-addicted client will not perform well at a deposition or on the witness stand. Because of memory problems and slow reactions, she may not remember the advice the lawyer gives immediately before the deposition. The client's stories may change. Under pressure, she may forget the focus and purpose of the lawsuit.

The only thing that the lawyer can do is spot this problem beforehand and suggest that the client request a dosage adjustment from his physician. Prozac cannot cure the pain of being fired from a job. Modern society—and the medical profession—seem to believe that a pill can wash away everyday pain. Unless a client is psychotic, talk therapy may help more than psychotropic medication.

Whenever possible, avoid representing clients who are currently using illegal drugs or who are alcoholics. Such avoidance may be impossible for the average criminal defense attorney. It is surprising, however, how many drug addicts walk into attorneys' offices and expect representation in disability cases or civil lawsuits. Drug addiction may be an illness, but the law gives it no such deference.

Mentally Ill Client

In the case of psychoses (where clients are out of touch with reality), drugs—modern pharmaceuticals—are a blessing. Many clients have mental problems, but at least some of those with psychoses such as schizophrenia and bipolar disorder admit to their disorders. When psychosis occurs, medication is absolutely necessary to reconnect the client with reality. The schizophrenic and the obsessive-compulsive cannot ignore the symptoms; they need medication in order to function in our society.

The clients with personality disorders, however, spend most of their time wallowing in denial. They realize that many people do not like them, but this seems normal. No fancy pill can cure them of being too intelligent and too intense. They may realize that depression plagues them half of the time, but taking Prozac isn't worth the weight gain. In short, people with personality disorders are normal enough to pass as sane.

Under the pressures of a divorce or a job loss, the personality disorder often flares up like an unsightly boil. The intensity of the emotions becomes overwhelming. The depressed person dissolves in tears most of the time. The borderline personality becomes obsessed with revenge. The lawyer needs to decide ahead of time how to deal with clients suffering from personality disorders. Firmness usually helps. It does the lawyer no good to get sucked into the emotion. Giving the client an abundance of encouragement can never do any harm. Also, clients who are overwhelmed by emotion usually benefit from strict direction. Do this, the attorney must tell them, and do it now!

Another problem is the person who thinks that violent behavior such as spousal abuse is normal and okay. A surprising number of these people exist. Because they were raised that way, they think the behavior is okay. The lawyer must avoid condemning the client, because condemnation will solve nothing. A better approach can be to point out that such behavior will only hurt the client. Insist that the behavior stop, immediately, and advise that the client engage in therapy.

Physically Ill Client

Physically ill clients succumb to three problems: depression, lack of caregivers, and malingering. Pain, and/or a sudden change in lifestyle, can drive disabled clients into depression. The person who can't work or can't move loses self-esteem fairly rapidly. The lawyer needs to recognize this and suggest appropriate action. Maybe the client needs to seek therapy. Have a list of therapists handy, as well as the numbers of the local mental health organizations.

Lawyers cannot do much for a client who lacks caregivers except expedite the process of obtaining relief. If the client is stuck in bed, make sure he or she telephones often. Hospitals have social workers who will need to be contacted if the sick patient is being left alone too often.

The malingering client is often hard to spot at first. Lawyers are not doctors, after all, and no one can measure the pain of another person. When the lawyer suspects that a client is malingering—faking illness in order to get disability benefits or higher damages—the best course is to bow out of the case gracefully as soon as possible. If you lose the case at the hearing stage, *refuse to file an appeal*. When and if a settlement opportunity occurs, encourage the client to accept it. If the client refuses to settle, end the attorney–client relationship. Make sure at all times that the retainer agreement allows the attorney to bow out of such situations "when the chance of winning is too slight."

Client Who Needs Multiple Services

Many clients who present themselves to lawyers are in big trouble and need a lot of help from various sources. They may be seeing several doctors, a therapist, and perhaps a chiropractor. They have financial problems that cause them to lose sleep. They're gaining weight at an alarming rate. They don't have health insurance and their children are sick.

The lawyer can only sit and listen to most of these woes. Sometimes a good listener is what the client needs more than anything. Often the attorney must be prepared to suggest therapists and certified public accountants, or public services that the client can obtain for free. Having a list of addresses and phone numbers available is an excellent strategy. For example, if a family with children lacks medical insurance even though the parents are working, how can it apply for reduced-price health insurance from the state? Is this service available? Where can the family apply?

All of the client's problems must be kept strictly confidential from the opposing side of the case and from the public at large. Enforce a strict containment policy. Secretaries and office clerks must realize that the clients' problems stay contained within the office. This is difficult sometimes, but resist the urge to joke about clients outside the office.

Persistent Client

Clients do exist who come in, pay their money for a divorce or other action, and never call the attorney on their own but wait to be called. These clients present their own sort of dilemma because they do not stay on top of the action. The attorney tends to shove these cases aside because the squeaky wheel gets the grease. But all in all, the absent client is preferable to the horribly persistent client.

The persistent client calls several times a day. He fills up the answering machine with phone messages. He may stop in at the attorney's office without notice, sit down, and wait for an impromptu conference. This happens, inevitably, when the attorney is preparing for court or working on an important brief with a midnight deadline.

The attorney must exercise anger control with persistent clients. Often the best way to do this is by setting limits. Only return phone messages when there is something to say. Excuse yourself from any telephone conversation when you are working toward a deadline. Refuse to talk for more than five minutes unless the client has an appointment. Refuse to see her at all when you are hurrying to court.

The persistent client needs lots of advice on dealing with third party professionals such as counselors, mediators, judges, and guardians *ad litem*. Establish rules for dealing with those professionals such as, "You can telephone the guardian, but only once. After that, wait for an emergency and call me

> **Smart Tip**
> Set limits as to when and under what circumstances you will answer phone calls and stick to those limits with every client. It would be easy for a small practitioner to spend all day on the telephone with clients. Don't do it.

first." Instruct the persistent client as to how to behave in court and during a mediation. Let the client know that you will cease your representation if the client refuses to obey. The client must, of course, answer any questions posed by the judge, but if he talks back to the judge or shows disrespect, you may refuse to represent him any further. The client must know this rule beforehand. The lawyer must have an "out" written into the retainer agreement to end his services if the client refuses to cooperate.

Humorous Client

The law is not a pretty profession, but it's often very funny. Lawyers who do not have a dark sense of humor should join a big firm and do tax law (although that may be hilarious, as well). You haven't lived until you've seen a 400-pound client run through your door yelling, "I need to use the bathroom!"

When a feisty female client calls to describe a fist fight in the employee lunch room with a female co-worker, the only thing to say is, "Excuse me while I laugh."

Clients say the strangest things. The other day I had a new client in my office, and parts of the conversation went like this.

Client: *Because of the narcolepsy, I'm not supposed to drive.*
Me: *How did you get here?*
Client: *I drove.*

Me: *You put the wrong date on this form.*
Client: *[Incredulous]. It's 2002???*

Client: *I drive my kids to school every day.*
Client: *The narcolepsy is kicking in. I think I'm falling asleep. Keep talking!*

Sometimes clients like these are the best medicine to get you through the day.

Clients on Stage: Depositions

One important reason client control is so important is that clients often need to present their cases—most frequently by giving depositions and sometimes, when it can't be avoided, in court. These situations are difficult for the most well-balanced person. For those who refuse to listen to their lawyers and have problems that make listening to their lawyer difficult, these moments on stage can be traumatic—and possibly fatal to their case, even a good case. Consider depositions.

Depositions are sworn statements, recorded by a court reporter and bound into a book format. The statements are taken with everyone sitting around a conference table, with the lawyers from all sides *and* all the clients present. The taking of a deposition is a highly-charged, emotional situation because the plaintiff or witness faces the person he is accusing and the questions from the lawyers are often quite pointed and heated. The lawyers do not pay much attention to hearsay rules when taking a deposition because they want to find out exactly what the party wants, what the witnesses know, and how much evidence everyone has. It is a direct fact-finding part of discovery, which lets both parties know what the other's strategy will be and how well the parties and witnesses will behave in court.

Clients behave differently under questioning. Some talk too much and spend pages and pages answering a simple query. Others give angry, staccato answers. The skillful deponents ponder each question and give a thoughtful response that manages to argue their side of the case every step of the way. For example:

Defense attorney: *Why did you choose to quit your job?*

Skillful client: *I did not choose to quit. I was forced out of my job as a librarian—a job I had trained for and aspired to all my life—because my boss would not promote me to the position of research librarian. He said that women should not be supervisors. I deserved the job, and so I quit after telling him that he was discriminating against me.*

Defense attorney: *Answer the question, please.*

Skillful client: *I have answered the question. If you want, we can have the court reporter read back my answer.*

Defense attorney: *Wouldn't you say, hypothetically, that the boss has the right to hire the person best-suited for the job?*

Skillful client: *I can only testify about my own situation. The head librarian discriminated against me, did not consider me for the job, because I am female. He told me that was the reason . . .*

Defense attorney: *But, in general, wouldn't you say that the boss can hire the person he or she wants for the job?*

Skillful client: *I can only answer questions about my own job.*

Clients almost never answer skillfully. They become tired and succumb to answering the hypotheticals. They give clipped answers in order to finish the deposition as quickly as possible. They become angry and refuse to answer completely. Or they become terrified and agree to everything suggested by the defense attorney, allowing the attorneys to lead them "down the garden path." It is almost impossible to tell in advance which type of error the client will make under pressure.

Attorneys need to prepare their clients for depositions in every way possible. Hold a practice question-and-answer session. Give the client a deposition tape to watch. Take them to observe other depositions in the case before their own occurs. Do whatever it takes to reduce the client's stress.

11

Theories about Practicing Law

Practicing law is a job of such social significance and focus in today's world that the small practitioner can really make a difference in her or his community. The cases you accept and those you turn down have a direct impact on which laws are enforced in your area. Any lobbying an attorney chooses to engage in might be more successful than the lobbying done by a lay person, simply because lawyers know something about how the courtroom operates. The way you treat your clients directly shapes the perception of lawyers—the picture lawyers present to the public. And because you're a solo or in a small partnership, you can develop the road map as to how you wish to conduct business.

Therapeutic Jurisprudence

Therapeutic jurisprudence is a relatively new concept that focuses on how the law and legal proceedings affect people emotionally and how the law impacts people's behavior and self-esteem. This concept, explored in depth by such legal scholars as David Wexler, professor of law and professor of psychology at the University of Arizona, is especially important to the small practitioner.

Preparing the Client

The attorney's first priority is preparing the client for mediation, depositions, and/or court appearances. When any lawyer invites a client to initiate a lawsuit against, say, a spouse or a former employer, it becomes that lawyer's responsibility to inform the client fully of the emotional devastation that such a legal action can cause. If the client decides to proceed anyway, the lawyer must prepare the client for every step of the process. This preparation includes descriptive warnings of all the bad things that could happen and how best to handle each situation.

For the small practitioner, who has close physical and telephone contact with each of his clients for years at a time, the obligation to prepare the client becomes even more evident than for the lawyer in a large firm. It's easy to become attached to clients in ways that lawyers at larger firms could never imagine. You are face-to-face with your clients without so many of the big-firm barriers: paralegals, secretaries, receptionists. Because there is more opportunity for the lawyer to talk with clients, there should be more opportunity to warn, explain, and discuss the situation to find out how that particular client, with his emotional sensibility, is likely to react to being in court or testifying at a deposition. Some clients are thick-skinned. Some are quiet and sensitive.

Every family court attorney knows that child custody cases are tough. The emphasis should always be on settlement. But when parties cannot agree, there will be fights over visitation rights with the children, arguments over child support, and disgust that the other parent is not buying the child clothing. There are the complaints that one parent is not letting them talk on the telephone to the other parent, problems with the grandparents, issues over school attendance or medical treatment. It can be endless.

Preparing the client for all of these problems may be impossible, but the lawyer must make an attempt. Describing the problems beforehand may convince the client to think harder about settlement. In states where the client faces a long divorce process, the agony will last for several months if the parties cannot find common ground. When the parties are emotionally unstable, the agony may last for the rest of their lives.

> **Smart Tip**
>
> As a small office practitioner, your top priority will be to explain the process to your client and prepare her for what lies ahead. What will happen in court? What are the possible consequences? List the reasons why settlement is always preferable. Make sure the client understands.

Revenge needs to be discouraged in these situations, even if a long, drawn-out divorce with its haggling over every issue could line the attorney's pockets. It is the lawyer's job to have a good head on her shoulders and discourage the parties from attempting to destroy each other. The lawyer who fuels the fire is failing to keep her client's emotional well-being in mind. She is failing to do her job.

Small practitioners often represent plaintiffs, the parties who sue. If a client seems to have a good lawsuit at hand, the lawyer needs to ensure that the client does not enter the legal arena blindfolded. If the client was terminated from his job, for example, a lawsuit means that the client will be reliving that termination for the next 18 months. His weaknesses as an employee may stand out. The employer's attorney will question the employee's veracity, his memory, and his value as a worker. And all of this will occur at depositions, unsupervised by judges, before the client sees the inside of a courtroom. Most people considering a lawsuit are not aware that their own lives will be distorted and placed under the microscope. Once again, the lawyer must give a realistic description of the typical lawsuit of this type—not just the trial itself, but the lengthy preparation, the depositions, and the time and money the client will be required to invest. The secret is the preparation.

Clients and witnesses should be prepared for depositions and for appearances in court. Because depositions are often boring to defend when your client is under interrogation, attorneys sometimes make the mistake of under preparing the witness or even allowing the client to attend alone. No one should ever attend a deposition alone, and no one should undergo a deposition without extensive preparation beforehand.

Dennis P. Stolle and Mark D. Stuaan explore the serious impact of depositions in their article "Defending Depositions in High-stakes Civil and Quasi Criminal Litigation: An Application of Therapeutic Jurisprudence," *Western Criminology Review*,

4(2), 2003 (http://wcr.sonomoa.edu/v4n2/stollestuaan.html). All depositions are emotionally draining, not just those described by Stolle and Stuaan. Much of the deponent's life is up for examination in a deposition, including many areas that would be declared irrelevant during an actual trial. Depositions should be nothing more than information-gathering exercises staged with a court reporter present to record the proceedings while the deponent is under oath. Unscrupulous attorneys, however, let loose in that sort of setting because no judge is present in the room. They use depositions to intimidate the opponent. Without an attorney, the deponent, inexperienced in the law, has little power to object to questioning, to telephone the judge, or to walk out if the situation becomes ridiculous.

> **Bright Idea**
> One key to practicing law in a small office is taking enough time to prepare your clients and witnesses for any court appearance. Prepare them for depositions by going over long sets of possible questions.

Handling Emotions

Small law offices have an obligation to be aware of their clients' emotional situations and to help in any way possible. Emotional hot spots could involve the client's family situation, her medical problems, or her inability to work. A client may have experienced the recent death of a child, for example. This experience could color every aspect of the client's life, including her legal problems. The good practitioner will know if something as important as this has befallen the client.

Emotions really flare up when a client is incarcerated. Attorneys must deal with the possibility of incarceration whether the attorney handles civil cases or criminal defense cases. Clients can be incarcerated for failure to pay child support, for driving when their licenses are under suspension, for simple possession, or for any of a wide variety of everyday events unconnected with the work being performed by the attorney.

The first person the family calls is the attorney, whether or not the attorney has any power at all to release the client from jail. The family might ask the attorney to pay the client's bail, to represent him at the bail bond hearing, or the try to get the client's medications to him. Even when there is very little the attorney can do, the correct response is to show compassion and (especially) be realistic. In the spirit of therapeutic jurisprudence, the attorney should not turn away completely. It would be unwise to say, "I warned the client to pay her child support obligation, and now there is nothing at all I can do." The attorney may say, "I can't prevent the client from serving her sentence, this time, but I can put in a motion for reduction of child support."

Or, "She needs a criminal defense attorney, and here are some good ones I can recommend." Never agree to pay a client's bail or lend a client money. This is a sure path to financial ruin and will not do the client any real good.

> **Smart Tip**
> Get to know your client's family situation and emotional strengths. Discuss any fears about testifying in court or at a deposition.

Another emotionally significant situation that a small office practitioner often faces is a client with a serious physical or mental illness. The first question with either of these situations is, whether the client has any relatives or friends who are supportive. When the client with a severe heart problem, for example, has a supportive adult child who might show up in the attorney's office or appear as a witness at a disability hearing, the attorney has much less to worry about. The adult child will take care of the client's physical and emotional needs, and the lawyer only has to perform her job. There may be more telephone calls from such a client, but all in all, the supportive child will be doing most of the therapeutic work.

When, on the other hand, a severely mentally ill client has been abandoned by his family or has a family far away, the lawyer has a greater responsibility. The lawyer needs to record the phone numbers and addresses of any relatives and keep in contact with them. These relatives need to be kept informed of the client's needs and condition, whether they like it or not. Make sure the client agrees to this beforehand. It might be a good idea to have the client sign a release stating that his legal matters and medical matters can be revealed to one or more relatives. If one of these distant relatives tends to be responsive at all, the attorney will have much less of a burden.

If there are no relatives willing to help, there is not much the attorney can do except do his job and listen to the client's complaints. Certain social services might be available, such as Meals on Wheels, but these often require money that the client may not have. If a medical social worker is involved, maybe through the hospital, make contact with that professional and ask for help.

The attorney must be a good explainer and an even better listener. Be ready for lengthy phone conversations and even longer meetings. Most clients are looking for conversation as well as legal advice. If they're in trouble or sick, they need someone to listen to their problems. Talking about problems makes them seem less serious. The compassionate practitioner meets that emotional need.

Assessing the Law

Another assessment that the lawyer can make is how certain laws, as they are written in the statutes, regulations, and cases, affect people psychologically. The legislature in South Carolina, for example, in recent years tried to give its employees more rights by writing into statutory law that employees who were let go (or terminated) had to be paid wages due to them by the time the next payroll went out. This statute, and other statutes in that section of the South Carolina Code, gave employees the emotional edge, causing them to feel less resigned to the situation in a union-free economy. Maybe employees *would* be treated fairly in South Carolina, at least as far as wages were concerned. The next wave of legal activity favored employers, who wanted to obliterate that law through the use of personnel handbooks. Handbooks were not to be considered contracts between employer and employee, but they did give employers the right to set the rules. If employees were terminated "for cause," their wages could be withheld, as long as it said so in the personnel handbook. Cases along these lines tended to hand power back to the employer.

Citizens are more likely to flex their muscles and declare their rights if they believe society backs them up. The citizen's perception of the law sometimes matters as much as the actual wording of the law itself. Some men are still under the impression that women are more likely to obtain custody of children than men. This no longer seems to be true in South Carolina, at least. It is a perception that lingers from the past, but it does influence people's actions. Likewise, when citizens believe they have no rights as employees, they tend to act accordingly, to wait longer to complain about harassment and to accept losing their wages.

The solo practitioner or small office partner is in a position to observe people's behavior because of what they believe the law can do for them or how it fails them. Telephone inquiries are informative. Calls from prospective clients can often tell as much as conversations with actual clients. What happened? Why did you choose to take that action? Who kept you informed or intentionally left you in the dark? The small office practitioner is in an excellent position to lobby for change.

Shaping Public Policy

More than other professionals, attorneys have the opportunity to influence public policy based on real experience as to how particular laws and regulations affect the public. Attorneys see the effects of laws every day. They see how particular laws favor the wealthy, how children suffer because of this policy or that, and how the judicial system punishes the poor. When there is racism and sexism, attorneys deal with it daily. Any sort of unfairness in the system hits them in the face.

Small office practitioners can choose to involve themselves in lobbying and the legislative process more easily than attorneys working for large firms. They have control of their own time. When the state legislature is in session, the small office practitioner can set aside time to attend legislative sessions without having to get

> **The Whole Truth**
> Small office practitioners are in a good position to lobby and become involved in the legislative process, whether they do it for pay or to fight for what they believe.

permission for time off. They can also choose which side to root for, without offending anyone who controls them directly. Although there is always the possibility of offending judges by making a public stand on some issue, judges cannot punish an attorney for exercising his First Amendment rights outside the court. Judges can be fair or unfair, but they always have a bigger issue to deal with: whether or not their decisions will be appealed with any success.

Changing the Laws

The small office practitioner who deals with laws and regulations every day will soon come across certain situations that are patently unfair and that seem hopeless to change. For example, until a few years ago the South Carolina guardian *ad litem* system seemed untouchable—and unfair. When custody battles occurred, family court required the appointment of a guardian *ad litem* to represent the minor child or the children in court. The guardian, named by the family court judge, had a powerful say in custody decisions and an often large court-ordered fee parents were required to pay. Most often appointments were made from a short list kept by the judges. No statute or court rule governed the behavior of the guardians, how much could be charged, how much work had to be done, or what written reports had to be submitted to the judge. Although there were good guardians who did their work conscientiously for reasonable fees, cronyism, high fees, and fee padding were rampant. My own family court clients complained, but there was really little I could do. The situation appeared hopeless.

Finally, a guardian went too far. Wealthy clients were ordered to pay a huge sum to a guardian *ad litem*, even though the custody decision in the case was obviously ill-advised. By the time the case reached the South Carolina Supreme Court, the issue was in the public eye. The case was overturned, and the guardian's actions were criticized. A grassroots organization criticizing the poor work done by guardians *ad litem* and their lack of supervision spread across the state. Thousands of citizens telephoned their state senators demanding that the system be reformed or fees and actions regulated.

The legislature began hosting hearings on the issue in Columbia that were advertised in the newspapers. So many citizens showed up to listen and to relate their experiences that these hearings had to be expanded and held at larger locations throughout the state. After wrangling in the legislature, a statute was written that set some requirements for guardians *ad litem:* no criminal record, a certain amount of education, and some training. Judges had to set limits on their fees. There were weaknesses, of course, but the statute moved in the right direction. This case illustrates the power of the vote. When citizens want something to happen, they can make it happen.

The Benefits of Public Service

Small law firms profit immensely from a partner being elected to political office. City council, state legislature, school board—all of these offices bring recognition and authority to a small law office. Lawyers who double as politicians become known as skillful compromisers who can produce settlements in court. Politicians know how to bargain. Plus, politicians usually have the respect of the judges because they have shown they can be elected.

Law firms also profit from the advertisement that comes from serving in public office. Almost all advertisement is good. Any public appearance on television or in the newspaper will do the trick.

Having access to public officials—speaking their language—is yet another privilege enjoyed by the attorney. Lawyers who appreciate their privileges and act accordingly will often find more fulfillment in their work.

Behaving Well in Court

Good attorneys know how to mask their anger; excellent attorneys know how to control it and channel its energy. This syllogism rings strikingly true during courtroom proceedings. You can't blow up at anyone in the courtroom, especially not the judge. The judge reigns as king of the castle or the empress on her throne. Whatever the judge says is law, even if he tells you to go change your clothes or proceed directly to jail. The judge can chastise you or the opposing attorney, just like professors in law school. She's always right, (unless you can win on appeal, but that comes much later).

Staying Cool

A useful phrase to remember is "Thank you, Your Honor," which serves as a fitting close to any proceeding, whether you've just won a huge verdict or made a fool of yourself and your client. You may be appearing before that same judge again tomorrow, next week, or next month. The scenario will be different; the results may be different, and your heart may be singing a different tune. One sure thing about the judicial system is that it's changeable. Practicing law is like riding a roller coaster. When something bad happens, give yourself a limit of 24 hours to mourn before moving on to the next case.

The law is full of emotional clients and attorneys, which makes it even more sensible to remain aware of your emotions, especially in court. Say to yourself, "That attorney is using his friendship with the judge to sway the outcome of this case. This is making me really angry." Say it to yourself, write it down if you must, but don't allow that anger to control your actions inside the courtroom. Plan a way to expend your anger afterwards, such as working out in the gym, running, shopping until you drop, cleaning out the garage, or playing tennis. Write a motion to rule the other side in. Compose a 25-item request to produce. Try not to yell at the opposing attorney or at his friend, the judge. Angry actions inside the courtroom always come back to bite you, and they spell victory to the other side.

> **Smart Tip**
> Whatever happens in court, control your anger and thank the judge. Save your emotions for later, go home and exercise, or rent a *Terminator* film.

Admonitions to stay cool inside the courtroom cannot be repeated often enough, because it's a rule that is nearly impossible to follow during the first years of practicing law. This is partly because it is so difficult to predict what will happen during any courtroom appearance. There are too many human factors to consider. What did the judge eat for breakfast? Which arguments will the opposing attorney bring up? Is my client keeping secrets from me? Is the judge friendly with the opposing attorney? Have I failed to uncover the controlling case law? Will the judge use a procedural issue to throw out my motion?

How to Stay Cool

The new attorney can use several tactics to help control his emotions inside the courtroom.

- Prepare alternate arguments to present during the hearing. If your client cannot have custody of the children, can she have liberal visitation with them?

- Before the hearing, list several strategies to follow afterwards if your argument is unsuccessful. If your client fails to obtain custody, will you then make some discovery requests? Will you press harder to resolve the issues by agreement? Will you depose their witnesses?

- Prepare your client for the worst. Tell her, "This is what we desire to happen tomorrow in court. This is the worst that can happen." Explain to your client that courtroom hearings are always unpredictable. Reiterate that the best option is always settlement.

- Keep in mind that most courtroom hearings are but one step in the lengthy process of litigation. Win this hearing, lose the next one. That's how cases usually

> ## Taking Control
>
> Make preparations before the hearing to control your emotions in the courtroom:
> - ❍ List alternate things to ask the judge for if you lose the big argument. If your client can't have custody of the children, can she have more visitation than usual?
> - ❍ Prepare your client ahead of time for the worst that can happen.
> - ❍ Remember that most hearings are but one step in the lengthy process of litigation. Lose today; win tomorrow.
> - ❍ If you find yourself growing angry, imagine yourself as a spectator in the courtroom drama that is taking place. Is there any irony in the situation?

proceed. The road to a jury trial or final hearing is a long one, and after the final hearing there's usually an opportunity to appeal. When you lose something, take the allotted 24 hours to mourn. Then proceed to the next step. What can you do to ameliorate the situation? How many ways can the other side shoot himself in the foot?

- If you find yourself inside a hearing, with negative emotions creeping into your head, imagine yourself removed from the situation, perched on a high cloud or sitting in the rafters, observing the comedy of errors. What is the heart of the matter? How could you describe it in writing? Would any of this injustice make a good joke to tell your friends at lunch? Viewing the courtroom objectively allows you to regain your perspective and your composure.

In the end, justice sometimes prevails. Make sure that your client has a say in the matter. Give your client a voice in front of the judge. That is all the attorney can do. Half of the time you're going to win; half of the time you're going to lose.

Dress for Success

Winning or losing, attorneys should always look their best in court. This means suits, pressed shirts, and clean shoes. Certain male judges prefer female attorneys to appear before them wearing skirts and male attorneys to have short hair. This does not make any sense, but attorneys should learn which way the wind blows in their districts. Do what the judge wants. Don't endanger your client's case over an article of clothing or a ponytail.

Clients often ask their attorneys how to dress for a courtroom appearance. The safest thing to tell them is to dress for work or for a religious service. Dressing carefully and somewhat formally signifies respect for the law, and judges enjoy that. An easy way to bow down and show respect is to dress carefully and conservatively. Why miss this opportunity?

> **Smart Tip**
> Dress comfortably and conservatively for court. Advise your client to do the same. The courtroom is not a place for Hawaiian shirts.

Acknowledging the Court Reporter

Another good idea is to acknowledge the court reporter. She is the one who marks the exhibits and records the proceedings. She may work for this particular judge exclusively. Greet her, pick up her card before the hearing begins, if there is time. Should you be required to write the resulting order, you will need to know the name of the court reporter as well as the judge. Should you need a transcript of the proceedings, you will probably communicate directly with the court reporter.

Handicapped but Not Disabled

Anyone with a physical handicap that alters her appearance or limits her mobility should not be deterred from practicing law. According to one small practitioner who uses a wheelchair because of a spinal cord injury, there may even be advantages in front of a jury for someone who has a visible handicap. He feels that juries tend to pay more attention to his arguments because he is in a wheelchair. "They listen to you more carefully," he says. This particular attorney is well spoken, and it would be difficult to separate the power of his words from the impact of his wheelchair. Suffice it to say that this attorney does not feel that his handicap hampers him in the practice of law, rather the reverse.

From his demeanor, this attorney does not consider himself to be "handicapped." Maybe "disabled," but not much. He gets around with considerable agility in a manual wheelchair and plays tennis. He states that many of his clients forget that he uses a wheelchair and have told him so after dealing with him for a certain amount of time. This lawyer feels that a lot of advertising is important to draw the clients in. His large Yellow Pages advertisements feature photographs of him sitting in a chair and his associate attorney standing next to him. When he had a partner in the practice, they used the same format for advertisements: one sitting, one standing. The ads do not show that he uses a wheelchair.

> **The Whole Truth**
>
> An attorney with a visible handicap may actually compel more attention from a jury than other attorneys.

Unlike juries, judges do not pay much attention to the fact that this attorney is "handicapped." At least this particular attorney does not believe so. "Disability makes no difference to judges," he says. Judges are supposed to be unbiased and fair, and most of them have enough savvy to look past the disability of a representative. This attorney can remember one occasion in the past nine or ten years when he was late to a hearing because he went to the wrong courthouse. He stated the reason as he wheeled into the courtroom. The judge excused him for being ten minutes late, and the attorney surmised he got this special treatment (judges have precious little tolerance for lack of punctuality) because he was in a wheelchair. The wheelchair was not the reason for his tardiness, but he let the judge draw his own conclusions. Why not let his client benefit from this misconception?

Accessibility

Most courthouses in large cities are accessible to the handicapped. But if you haven't been there before, how can you be sure? When the aforementioned attorney prepares to travel to an unknown courthouse, he telephones the clerk of court ahead of time to find out if the place has the proper ramps and parking spaces. Once, the attorney was scheduled to try a case in a courthouse without handicap accommodations. "Look," he informed the clerk of court. "I have to get into this building." The clerk transferred the trial to a newer office building that was accessible to the handicapped. Luckily the attorney had given that clerk of court enough notice to make special arrangements.

State bar offices may publish information on which courthouses and hearing sites are handicapped accessible, where the parking spaces are, and other useful tidbits that could help an attorney with mobility problems.

And remember, attorneys often deal with clients who are themselves sick or disabled. Maybe the client is suing over a car accident. Maybe the client wants to get Social Security disability. What should the attorney do when the client looks less disabled than the representative? Attorneys will use every tactic they can to win an argument, and they won't stop short of using an opponent's handicap.

This attorney solves that problem by pointing to his client's education or lack

> **Smart Tip**
>
> Before traveling to an unfamiliar courthouse for a hearing, telephone the clerk of court ahead of time to obtain details about parking and wheelchair accessibility.

thereof. He feels that education is the key to success for a handicapped individual. Because attorneys enjoy much more education than most of the population, this argument can be used again and again, if the need for explanation arises. "I have the education to practice law, but this client of mine worked in a factory for ten years. Unless he finishes college and law school, he will not be in the same position I am. His lack of education is a major disability."

Conclusion: The Compleat Lawyer

The philosophy of therapeutic jurisprudence is an excellent philosophy for the small office practitioner to follow. This refers to the practical lawyer, the caring lawyer, the smart lawyer administering to her client as a whole person, with a mentality, a career, and a family, which all factor into the situation. This concept refers to solving problems rather than acting as a hired gun or threat to the opposing party. It means looking out for the welfare of both parties in divorce cases. It means advising a client to leave a particular job when the client is not suited for the work, rather than suing the company that is about to lay him off. It means finding suitable drug counseling for a client who is addicted, rather than insisting that she have custody of the children. It means looking hard at the big picture and giving good advice.

Acknowledging the Client's Stress

When a client presents himself for legal assistance with a divorce or a child custody battle, the client may also exhibit a need for psychological counseling and financial planning. I say "may," but probably 80 percent of divorce clients have an urgent need for both these services. Sometimes the client's situation of being on the edge creates the psychological stress and the financial woes. Sometimes it's the other way around. Whatever the reason, some litigants in family court requires counseling for fiscal and for psychological problems. The lawyer with a therapeutic approach may recognize the needs of the client more quickly than the lawyer with an assembly line approach. Any lawyer handling a divorce case needs to act like a case manager and consider the client's entire situation—not just how to get her divorced as quickly as possible. What will the client do for money after the divorce? Does the client have a support group of family and friends? How will the stresses of the divorce affect the client's job? Is the client addicted to drugs or alcohol?

The Client's Financial Problems

Clients often have financial problems. The current system in the United States does not promote the intelligent use of money. Financial responsibility is not taught in schools or the family. The overwhelming availability of credit and a must-have lifestyle combine to leave people without retirement reserves, without liquidity, and with huge amounts of debt. The most hunchbacked debt carriers usually belong to the upper middle class, often well-paid professionals. Usually they live very well (big house, double mortgage) and do not see themselves in the mirror until divorce forces them to reckon with their financial situation. The spouse leaves, and they catch a glimpse of themselves—Quasimodo, driving a Land Rover, $40,000 in debt. The credit card companies love it. Divorce lawyers see lots of pain.

The Client's Psychological Problems

Separation also places a magnifying glass on psychological problems. American society has many adults with mental illnesses. These illnesses—depression, bipolar disease, personality disorders—become magnified by divorce. Oftentimes in family courts, a psychologist is appointed by the judge to evaluate both the parties and any children, which works well if the psychologist makes strong recommendations and actually helps the parties resolve their differences. A psychologist who acts as a mediator can do wonders for resolving a case, just as a guardian *ad litem* who writes up a feasible plan for settlement can actually earn the money the parties are ordered to pay him.

All the authority figures involved in orchestrating a divorce—the lawyers, the judges, the guardians, and any other advisors—need to understand the prevalence of mental illness. It is a pervasive problem that can be crippling and may require drugs to move the client back into the mainstream.

Listening to the Client

Lawyers have the opportunity to listen to many aspects of their clients' lives—personal, medical, and financial. Because of this, lawyers have a more urgent duty than most professionals to look at their clients' problems from many angles. A good lawyer is not a hired gun. If one particular relative is causing estate problems, that relative must be called in and dealt with rather than treated as the enemy. If a client needs psychological counseling, he must be told so in no uncertain terms. If a family has no medical insurance, the lawyer has the obligation to seek out some Medicaid or another feasible solution. This requires networking and imagination.

A compleat lawyer must be a compleat person, someone who has empathy, and empathy involves realizing that clients are not problems but people with leisure lives and family lives. The lawyer who has family obligations recognizes what it means to care for children and the urgency of spending time with family.

Accepting the Responsibilities of the Law

Being a lawyer, an officer of the court, is a public service job and carries a tremendous amount of responsibility. In today's political climate, where lawyers (especially trial lawyers) are decried as enemies of the common good, the profession deserves a second look both by the public and by the lawyers themselves. It's easy to be swayed by the media into thinking that lawyers are bad, heartless people or that being cutthroat is the proper way to conduct business because that's what the public expects.

But lawyers are smart people. You don't have to be driven by a discriminatory picture of lawyers fueled by the media. You don't have to be underhanded just because that's what the other guy may do. You can think for yourself. You can be intuitive and see the big picture. Most of the time, you can discern the correct course of action. Sometimes you can actually do it.

Too often, of course, an attorney is required to be ruthless because the attorney on the other side is that way. The other lawyer has a vanity license plate that reads "Just Win." He neither sees the big picture nor cares how much damage he does. The guy won't compromise, ever. Under circumstances like these, the small office practitioner, no matter how intelligent, has no choice but to fight the long fight that is both a waste of time and public resources.

Sometimes, however, the attorney can see a clear way to improve both his client's life and his opponent's life. The problem is clear, and the solution is evident. The client may not completely agree, but the attorney can reason and describe things well enough to change the client's mind. The attorney knows she is right; she has no doubt. It would be possible to earn more money by carrying out a full-blown trial, but the attorney sees there is a better way. A small office practitioner has more freedom than anyone in a larger firm to take the right pathway. The small office practitioner is her own boss.

Maybe there is a law that drastically needs changing. The solo or small office partner sees clients every month who are suffering because of a particular law or regulation. The attorney can do something to help. Unfettered by billable hours and managing partners, the person who manages his own time can carve out a schedule that allows some attention to public policy. He can exercise his own politics without worrying about offending those above him.

By paying attention to the world at large, the small practitioner can do more than other lawyers to change the negative public persona that plagues attorneys. Small office practitioners can rip off that mask and reveal that attorneys do the public more good than many other professions. Whether they operate as watchdogs for civil rights, for small business owners, or for big corporations, lawyers usually have the best interests of their clients at heart.

If lawyers can take the binoculars off billable hours and pay attention to the best interests of society at large—give back to their communities—they can garner a more positive reputation. Lawyers are already practicing social work much of the time, anyway. Small office practitioners, who enjoy more choices than almost any other category of lawyer, can lead the way.

Appendix
Helpful Resources

They say you can never be too rich or too thin. While these could be argued, we believe "You can never have too many resources." Therefore, we present for your consideration a wealth of sources for you to check into, check out, and harness for your own personal information blitz.

These sources are tidbits, ideas to get you started on your research. They are by no means the only sources out there, and they should not be taken as the Ultimate Answers. We have done our research, but businesses—like customers—tend to move, change, fold, and expand. As we have repeatedly stressed, do your homework. Get out and start investigating.

Web Sites

In this age of computers, the newly launched solo practice will rely heavily on personal computers. Not only does the computer often take the place of an expensive paralegal, but through the internet, it provides the gateway to important legal forms, court schedules, and online filing. The following is a list of helpful web sites.

FindLaw (www.FindLaw.com). Administered by Westlaw®, this web site provides links to federal statutes and state statutes from every state. In addition, it has recent case law, both federal and state, and links to specialty areas such as bankruptcy and employment law. In the hands of the litigious general public, this web site is the enemy because it provides the means for research by laymen who may to misinterpret what they read.

For lawyers, however, FindLaw is an excellent way to begin research (print out a couple of cases before heading to the library) or obtain the latest version of a statute.

The Federal Court System (www.uscourts.gov). This web site is the gateway to federal district courts in your area, to appellate courts, and to the U.S. Supreme Court. A lawyer who is filing a case in federal court for the first time would follow the links to the district court in his area. That web site will have a list of forms, such as the federal summons, federal cover sheet, and federal subpoena, that will be necessary to carry out the case. Another resource is the local federal rules available for the attorney to print out and read before filing the case. Federal court has a strict set of timetables that differ from other court scenarios at lower levels. Federal court administration often requires the plaintiff's attorney to file answers to special discovery requests along with the summons and complaint. Without these answers to discovery, the attorney may be unable to file the complaint.

In order to print out the forms available on these local web sites, the lawyer should have Adobe Acrobat® Reader installed on his computer. I recommend purchasing the full version of Adobe Acrobat, which allows the attorney to fill out forms online. Although this costs much more, around $300, it eliminates the need for a typewriter because the forms can be filled out on the computer and then printed out.

AOL's Guide to Government (www.mygov.governmentguide.com). This is an excellent starting place for the lawyer who wants to lobby for certain types of legislation or is thinking of pursuing lobbying as a business. By plugging in your ZIP code plus four, you can find out who your legislators are and how they voted on various bills. If your legislator recently appeared in the news, the stories are provided. Most importantly, the site tells you how to contact your government representatives.

The National Association of Women Lawyers (www.nawl.org). This organization is working to develop a network of female attorneys, with special emphasis on female owners or partners in law practices. NAWL will send you a complimentary copy of its guide to female-owned law practices. It honors and supports women who work in the legal profession and sponsors CLEs featuring Supreme Court justices and other high-profile female attorneys.

Martindale-Hubbell (www.martindale.com). This company publishes the revered directory of law firms, which rates lawyers and law practices and gives short biographies of lawyers practicing in the United States. Martindale-Hubbell can be used by the new attorney to discover basic information about opposing counsel.

For attorneys who wish to build a web site, Martindale-Hubbell also provides canned web sites that are interesting because they include legal newsletters on various topics such as family law. These web sites are, perhaps, more readily searchable because of the links associated with Martindale-Hubbell.

Within Martindale-Hubbell, there is a link to www.lexisONE.com, which allows free searches of case law. The search engine is easy to use and will only give you results if the parameters of the search (date, key word, relevant court) are narrow enough to bring up 100 cases or less.

American Bar Association (www.aba.net). Membership in the American Bar Association may be a waste of money unless the small practitioner plans to establish a high profile among attorneys nationwide. Many small office lawyers are more interested in establishing a profile within their own state. The ABA offers big-time continuing legal education courses, a library of practice manuals, and the chance for nationwide leadership roles.

Lawyers Weekly *(www.Lawyersweekly.com). Lawyers Weekly* (South Carolina edition) arrives at my office every week, even though I never purchased a subscription. It is a welcome sight, and I usually find articles of interest. These articles are synopses of recent cases, along with a photo of one of the lawyers involved. The year-end listing of the most important cases is something that I clip out and save. The weekly edition always includes synopses on employment law and family law, two areas of my practice. I also read the advertisements for mediation and other legal services.

The web site for this newspaper provides links to states where *Lawyers Weekly* publishes state editions. This is a useful publication, and I hope they are able to expand throughout the United States.

Social Security Web Site (www.ssa.gov). As with the federal court web site, this site is a way to obtain necessary forms. Some of the forms can be filled out on the computer, but usually I just print them out for my client's signature. Some of the forms can be filed online.

Clients can apply for Social Security disability benefits through this web site, register a name change, and do other necessary chores. The web site includes a form to request Social Security speakers for your organization. It also answers questions about the Social Security system.

Start-Up Office Supplies

Office machines are an expensive part of your start-up costs, so have another attorney advise you what brand of machines to buy and the software you'll need. It's best to have two working computer set-ups (computer and printer), but in the first year, one set-up will do.

Besides furniture, such as a desk, chairs, and conference table, here is a bare bones list of materials to buy for the beginner's office.

- Computer
- Jump drive, CD burner, and CD discs
- Microsoft Word or Word Perfect
- Adobe Acrobat to read/create PDF files
- Quicken or some other easy accounting software
- Ink jet printer
- Fax machine
- Scanner
- Desk-top copier that can handle a stack of 25 pages
- Two letter-size file cabinets, 4 drawers each (can be purchased used)
- Letter-size accordion folders
- Letter-size manila folders
- Scissors
- Two staplers (regular size)
- One heavy-duty stapler that can handle up to 60 pages
- Printed envelopes
- Ink stamp with address of office
- Letterhead stationery (unless you want to print it yourself)
- 9 x 11 envelopes
- 10 x 12 envelopes
- Postal scale
- Postage stamps
- Business cards
- Business card holders
- Telephone with speaker capability
- Three-ring binders
- Three-hole punch
- Post-It® notes and dispenser
- Paper clips and butterfly paper clips
- Paper for printer and copier
- Pens
- Markers
- Pen holders

- Calculator
- Tape and tape dispenser
- Briefcase (small, soft-sided, for every day)
- Briefcase (large, for trials)

Glossary

Administrative proceeding: Grievance brought before a body lower than or outside of the local, state, and federal court systems. Workers' compensation hearings are administrative proceedings.

Affidavit: A sworn statement, with notarized signature, prepared for use in court.

Answer: Pleading filed in court by the defendant to respond to the initial complaint in a lawsuit.

Appeal: Action brought in a higher (appellate) court to reverse or change a decision made in a lower court.

Arbitration: Procedure like a trial, which occurs outside the court system, in which an arbitrator issues a decision. The decision can be appealed unless the arbitration is *binding*.

Brief: Legal and factual argument prepared by an attorney in a case and possibly filed in court.

Case law: Decisions written in cases by judges at the trial or appellate level that interpret statutes or previous case law.

Civil action: Lawsuit or grievance brought between two private parties to resolve a dispute. Divorces and automobile accident cases are civil actions.

Clerk of court: Person, sometimes an elected official, who is in charge of the filing, storage, and retrieval of court records, such as pleadings.

Complaint: Initial pleading, asking for certain types of relief, filed with the court to initiate a lawsuit.

Contingency fee: Attorney's fee, usually a percentage of a settlement or judgment, which the attorney receives if the case is won or settled.

Court reporter: Person trained to record sworn testimony, either inside or outside the courtroom.

Criminal action: Proceeding brought by the government against a private party for committing an offense of a public nature.

Defendant: The party who is sued in a lawsuit.

Deposition: Written record ("transcript") of sworn testimony taken outside the courtroom before a court reporter, with the attorneys and parties present.

Discovery: Gathering evidence by requesting documents, issuing interrogatories (questions) to the opposing side, taking depositions, and issuing subpoenas before a case goes to trial.

Escrow account: Bank account used by an attorney to hold clients' money.

Guardian *ad litem*: Person appointed by the court to represent a minor child or incapacitated person (such as a prisoner) during a court case.

Mediation: Structured settlement meeting, presided over by a mediator who tries to facilitate settlement but does not issue a decision.

Plaintiff: The party who initiates a lawsuit.

Pleadings: Paperwork such as the complaint, answer, motion, certificate of service, etcetera, which is filed with the court during a lawsuit.

***Pro se* litigant:** Party who represents himself in a lawsuit, without an attorney.

Retainer: Fee charged by the attorney before starting work on a case, which usually covers a certain number of hours' work.

Roster: List of cases which the court is preparing to call for trial.

Statutes: Laws, made and written by the government at the federal, state, and local levels.

Summons: Pleading used to begin a civil action, which usually gives the defendant a certain amount of time to file an Answer or otherwise respond.

Index

A

A-type personality as suited to solo practice, 5
Accepting the responsibilities of the law, 101–102
Accessibility as major selling point, 20–21
Accountants
 relationships with, 60–61
 services of, 24, 30
Accounting
 programs, 73
 systems, 29–30
Addicted client, 80–81
Advertising, 38–40
 honesty as best form of, 66
 telephone book, 38, 39
 to avoid, 39–40
 web site, 40
Yellow Pages, 39–40
Appendix, 103–107
Arbitration, 55
Assessing the law, 92

B

Balancing the books, 73
Bank accounts, 29–30
Basic forms, building a computer file of, 30
Behaving well in court, 94–97
Big dogs, fighting against the, 4
Billing with complete honesty, 11
Borrowing money, 36
Build a life you love to live, 74
Business license, 24

C

Case
 files, creating, closing and storing, 45–47
 keeping it alive after filing, 47–48
 loads, avoiding unwieldy, 72
 managing a, 44–49
Change, being a force for, 6–8
Changing the laws, 93–94

Charges, determining your fees, 37–38
Children's toys in your office, 21
Choosing the right areas of practice, 14–17
    questions to ask yourself, 14–15
Clerks of court, relationships with, 62–63
Clerks, avoid depending upon law, 3
Client
    compound, 78–79
    files, setting up and maintaining, 25–27
    humorous, 84
    malingering, 82
    mentally ill, 81–82
    money, don't steal, 10–11
    persistent, 83–84
    physically ill, 82
    preparing the, 88–90
    representing your, 75–85
    screening the, 72
    sick, 80
    stress, acknowledging, 99–100
    vengeful, 77–78
    walk-in, 21
    who thinks he's a lawyer, 76–77
    with psychological problems, 100
Client control, 76–84
    and settlements, 48–49, 53
Clothes, 4, 96–97
Compleat lawyer, the, 99–102
Computers and their programs, 27
Conflicts of interest, avoiding, 13
Connections, developing, 64–66
Copiers, 27–28, 37
Court
    behavior, 94–97
    reporter, acknowledging, 97
    tactics for staying cool in, 95–96
Courthouse
    handicap accessibility, 98–99
    proximity to, 22

D

Dead snakes, evildoers and lawyers, 10
Defendant's attorney, 3
Deposition
    as client on stage, 84–85
    fees, 38
Discovery responses, 31
Doctors, relationships with, 58–59
Dress for success, 96–97
Dual degrees, 58

E

Emotions, handling, 90–92
Empathy, 101
Employees, 34–35
    and employment laws, 35
    never hire an ex-client, 35
Escrow accounts, client, 11, 29

F

Family attorney as first line of defense when landing themselves in serious trouble, 8
Family photographs as nice personal touch in office, 20
Fee-agreements, 37
Files, creating, closing and storing case, 45–47
Financial management, staying in charge of, 73
Financial problems, client's, 100
Financing, 36–37
Forms, building a computer file of, 30
Frivolous lawsuits from disgruntled clients, 25
Frugality, 33–40

G

General practitioner as too broad, 14
Get a life, 71–74
Getting started, 23–31
Glossary, 109–110

H

Handicapped but not disabled attorney, 97–98

Index

Help people, solo practitioners must have a strong desire to, 6
Home office, 21–22
Hourly rates, 37
Humorous client, 84

I

Income
  first year's, 37
  necessity of secondary source for solo practitioners, 5–6
Incorporating, 24
Integrity, setting the standard for, 11
Internet
  advertising, 40
  and the library, using the, 67–69
  connections, 28
Internships, 2

L

Law books, purchasing for your office, 28–29
Law enforcement officials, relationships with, 61
Law library, 67–69
Law school
  relevance of, 1–4
  tough and competitive nature of, 4
  what they don't teach you in, 41–49
Laws, changing the, 93–94
Legal research, 67–69
Liability insurance, 24–25
Library and the Internet, 67–69
Listening to the client, 100–101
Listening to your heart and pocketbook when choosing areas in which to practice, 14
Lobbying and involvement in legislative process, 92–93
Location and its effect on how your practice takes shape, 20, 21
Losses teach valuable lessons, always move forward, 2
Luck matures into experience in choosing areas of practice, 17
Lucrative relaxation, third choice, 16

M

Malingering client, 82
Managing a case, 44–49
Mediation, 49, 54–55
Mentally ill client, 81–82
Mentors, finding true, 14, 17, 42–44
  among your neighbors, 20
Money problems, clients with, 79–80
Mother-daughter compound client, 79
Multiple services, client who needs, 82–83
Myths, dispelling lawyer, 10–13

N

Networking, benefits of, 63–64
Non-work activities, scheduling, 73–74

O

Office
  equipment, 25–28, 36–37
  furnishing your, 20, 36
  style, projecting an image, 20
  supplies, start-up, 105–107
  your, 19–22
Old standard, second choice, 15–16
Online research, 67–69
Overcharging, avoid, 11

P

Paralegal
  avoid depending upon, 3
  forgoing, 34
Partnerships, pros and cons of, 8–10
Passion, first choice, 15
Payment upfront, 37
Peers, your, 63
People and their problems, ability to listen and empathize with, 5, 6
Persistent client, 83–84
Personal days, scheduling, 74
Physically ill client, 82

Plaintiff's attorney, 3
Playing well with others, 57–66
Pleadings, keeping a library of, 30
Power, don't misuse your, 11–12
Practicing law, theories about, 87–102
Preparing the client, 88–90
Printers, 27
Pro se opponents, avoid taking advantage of, 11–12
Professionals
    relationships with legal, 62–66
    relationships with other, 57–61
Psychological problems, client's, 100
Public policy, shaping, 92–93
Public service, benefits of, 94

Q
Quicken, 29, 73

R
Real world roles may be determined by personality, grades and connections made in law school, 3–4
Receptionist, hiring a, 34
Record-keeping, 25–28
Reinventing oneself, prerogative of solo practitioners, 17
Relationships
    law school as tough on familial, 4
    with legal professionals, 62–66
    with other professionals, 57–61
Research skills as basic reconnaissance tactics every law student must master, 2–3
Resources, helpful, 103–107
Retainer, 37–38
    agreement, 45, 76
Ridicule, how to withstand, 2

S
Self discipline as prerequisite for solo work, 5
Setting your own hours, 4
Settlement
    as best option in most cases, 48–49
    negotiated, 53–54
    outside of court, 51–55
Sick client, 80
Social workers, relationships with, 60
Solo practitioner
    enables one-on-one client contact and a host of other advantages, 4
    having the right stuff to become a, 4–8
    rules for, 5–8
State bar's lawyer referral service, 39
Staying cool in the courtroom, tactics for, 95–96
Steady income not a guarantee in solo practice, 4–5
Stress, acknowledging client's, 99–100
Summer jobs, 2

T
Teachers, finding, 15–16
Telephone
    book ads, 38, 39
    systems, 28
Temporary help, 34
Theories about practicing law, 87–102
Therapeutic jurisprudence, 88, 99–101
Therapists, relationships with, 60
Time management for work, 72–73
Truth, stick to the, 12

V
Vengeful client, 77–78
    protecting yourself from, 78

W
Walk-in clients, 21
Web site, creating your own, 40
Web sites, list of helpful, 103–105
Work overload, avoiding, 72
Working on your own, 5

Y
Yellow Pages ad, 39–40